EASY KETO

This book is dedicated to everyone who is looking to take their health into their own hands.

EASY KETO

PETE EVANS

70+ SIMPLE AND DELICIOUS RECIPES

RECLAIM YOUR HEALTH WITH A KETOGENIC DIET

plum. Pan Macmillan Australia

CONTENTS

INTRODUCTION

There has been a lot of hype lately about the ketogenic diet and I wanted to do something that would make adopting this approach to eating feel easy, accessible and, most importantly, delicious. And that's what inspired me to write *Easy Keto* – a simple handbook that delivers only the nutritious essentials you need to go keto. In short, it's designed to give you the tools to transition to a new way of eating that will train your body to burn fat for fuel. I believe that going keto is one of the best ways we can promote optimal health. By learning to cook and eat the right ingredients, you allow your body to regain its metabolic flexibility so that it can burn both glucose and fat.

I began following a mild ketogenic diet after I read *Primal Body, Primal Mind* by Nora Gedgaudas close to a decade ago. Since then, I've followed a paleo approach to life with an emphasis on cycling in and out of a mild state of ketosis. The two biggest differences I notice about eating keto are the increase in my energy levels and the improvement in my cognitive function – most noticeably my clarity of thought, recall and focus. But perhaps the coolest thing is that eating good-quality keto food makes me feel fuller for longer.

At its core, going keto is about embracing a diet that is lower in carbs and higher in healthy fats in order to allow your body to switch on its ability to burn fat for fuel. I like to think of going keto as cycling through a routine of eating, feasting and fasting: consistently eating a low-carb, high-fat and moderate-protein diet; occasionally feasting by increasing your carb intake; and fasting intermittently if it works for you (for more on this, see page 15). All of my food is paleo first and foremost, so I always steer well clear of processed foods and foods that can most commonly cause inflammation – grains, legumes and dairy. Instead, I eat good-quality proteins and fats from well-sourced land and sea animals, adding some low-carb vegetables, as well as fermented foods and bone broths made from organic ingredients whenever possible.

Even though we have been hearing a lot about the ketogenic diet in recent years, it's actually nothing new. In fact, the name has been around since the 1920s, when some doctors used it to treat patients with conditions, such as type 1 diabetes, epilepsy and neurological disorders. In reality, this dietary approach, in which we mainly lived on the fat and protein of the animals we hunted, has kept the human race evolving for millions of years.

However, in the modern Western world, most people don't have that kind of diet and, as a result, are not enjoying optimum health, and in some cases have lost the ability to burn fat altogether. By moving in and out of ketosis for several months, you can re-ignite your primal ability to burn fat for fuel. And if you continue on this regimen, it will help you gain better health. Not only does going keto turn on our fat-burning switch, giving sustained weight loss and enhanced energy, but the latest nutritional science shows that it may be a powerful way to manage metabolic disorders and keep our hormones balanced.

I've been road-testing the low-carb, healthy fats lifestyle for a number of years now and I find the more consistent I am with what and when I eat, the more energy I have to live my life. Now, in this book, I'm hoping to share some of this abundant energy with you.

I've included the information I've found most useful in my own journey and have developed more than 70 recipes to inspire you to get in the kitchen and cook healthy keto meals. I know you'll want to dive right in and get started with overhauling your pantry, so I've included guidelines for keto-friendly food swaps and how to build a keto pantry. Plus there's helpful information on supporting your health journey, such as how to avoid the keto slump and testing for ketones.

As always, I encourage you to track your own health journey to find out what works best for you. Some people respond better to a full ketogenic approach; others enjoy greater health by staying in a mild ketogenic state; while others prefer to cycle in and out weekly, monthly, seasonally or yearly. Whichever approach you take, the keto diet will help you to switch on your body's innate ability to burn fat in order to lose weight, have more energy and reach optimal health.

Cook with love and laughter,

PETE EVANS

HOW TO GO KETO

WHAT IS KETOSIS?

Our body has two primary sources of fuel: glucose and fat. When we eat a diet that is high in carbohydrates, our body converts the carbohydrates into glucose and uses that to provide the energy it needs to function. If, however, we significantly reduce the level of carbohydrates in our diet, our body will switch to burning fat for energy – a state known as ketosis. When our body is in ketosis, the liver converts fatty acids into molecules called ketone bodies, which then travel to the brain where they are used as the main source of energy. And this, in a nutshell, is what going keto is all about: eating a diet that is low in carbs, relatively high in healthy fats and with a moderate amount of protein, and perhaps combining it with regular fasting. Eating this way deprives the body of glucose and forces it into ketosis, when it burns fat instead of glucose as its main source of fuel.

KETOSIS VS KETOACIDOSIS

When looking into a ketogenic diet people sometimes confuse the healthy process of ketosis with ketoacidosis – a dangerous condition that occurs most commonly in people with diabetes. This condition is a dangerous metabolic state that can arise when insulin levels are not managed properly, leading to extremely high levels of ketones in the blood.

Ketosis, on the other hand, is a safe process where fat is used as the primary source of fuel in the body. In ketosis, ketones are released into the blood in a much smaller concentration and instead of accumulating (like in ketoacidosis) they are used up as an energy source.

HIGH-CARB DIET

High-carb intake causes glucose levels to rise

Pancreas releases insulin into bloodstream

Insulin allows glucose to enter cells

Fast-burning energy

KETO DIET

Fewer carbs and more fat in diet: glucose levels fall

Lipase hormone causes fatty acid release from fat stores

Fatty acids broken down in liver to ketones

Sustained energy

WHY SHOULD I GO KETO?

The ketogenic diet is a tool that can be used throughout your life to support better health. It can have a whole range of benefits, such as burning body fat and helping to lose weight, improving mental clarity and providing sustained energy.

But it also does far more than this. Going keto can help to manage metabolism, because when you eat healthy fats and enough protein, and minimise your carb intake on a daily basis, it can cause a significant reduction in hunger. This is because fat is abundant in our bodies, even in someone with a slight build, so once we switch over to burning fat for energy, there is a steady supply of fuel as long as we maintain a healthy diet. It is also due to the positive effect that fats and protein have on appetite-controlling hormones.

The keto diet might also be able to help prevent and manage some metabolic disorders. These include inflammatory disorders, such as polycystic ovarian syndrome as well as obesity, type 2 diabetes and cardiovascular disease. And it has been used to help treat children suffering from epilepsy. In fact, before anti-epileptic drugs were developed, the ketogenic diet was the standard epilepsy treatment from the 1920s.

Going keto makes it easier to keep the hormones insulin and leptin balanced and operating correctly. Insulin is released by the pancreas to keep blood sugar at appropriate levels. Eating too many carbs can lead to increased levels of insulin, which in turn can lead to the body becoming resistant to insulin. When following a keto diet, you naturally keep your level of carbohydrates low and this means that insulin should be able to function normally. Meanwhile, leptin is a key hormone that helps to regulate our appetite. However, our bodies can also become leptin resistant, mostly as a result of a diet high in sugar- and starch-based carbohydrates, which means that we are more likely to eat more often and overeat. Decreasing your carbohydrate intake and increasing your healthy fat and protein intake will help you to stabilise your leptin levels and allow you to enjoy more energy and a focused mind.

Think of going keto as a way to bring balance back to your body, mind and soul through the food you eat and the lifestyle you choose.

THE BENEFITS OF GOING KETO

- Improved cognitive health
- Reduced appetite and decreased cravings
- Reduced risk of chronic diseases
- Balanced hormonal health
- Improved metabolism

CHOOSE YOUR KETOGENIC APPROACH

Each of us is different and it's important to find what works best for you. There are five main types of ketogenic approach. The first is full ketogenic or a standard ketogenic diet, where about 70% of your energy comes from fat, 25% protein and 5% carbs. Some people stay in this very low carbohydrate lifestyle (about 20–50 grams of net carbs per day) and remain in ketosis the whole time. Certain medical conditions require this and for some this works best for their bodies.

The second approach is cyclical ketogenic, which means to cycle in and out of ketosis. In this popular method, people first enter ketosis by limiting their carbs to 20–50 grams of net carbs per day for a period of time. They then break out of ketosis by increasing their net carbs to anywhere up to 150 grams for a day, before returning to their original level of carbs. This can be repeated weekly, fortnightly or monthly. Some people like to mimic our hunter–gatherer ancestors and cycle in and out of ketosis slowly though the year. As the warmer months approach and the fruit is ripening, they slowly increase their carb intake, then ease back into a state of ketosis and burn fat for fuel through the cooler months.

The third approach, which is what I personally do, is to stay in a state of mild ketosis, fluctuating in and out as my body sees fit. I don't count carbs but generally eat very low carb to lower carb with the occasional higher intake of carbs when I feel like it, without being regimented or following a strict plan. When I do increase my carbs, they always come from healthy sources, such as higher carb vegetables like sweet potatoes or parsnips, avoiding dairy, grains, legumes and refined sugars.

The fourth approach is known as a targeted ketogenic diet, and it is one that is popular with athletes and fitness enthusiasts. In this approach, you eat all of your carbs for the day either before or after exercising. This gives your muscles a burst of energy for training. Meals at other times of the day have very few or even no carbohydrates.

Finally, some people follow a high-protein ketogenic diet (or carnivore diet), in which less than 10 grams of net carbs are consumed per day. In this approach, about 35–45% of your energy comes from protein, 55–65% from fat and almost none from carbs. For some this seems to help reduce appetite and gut inflammation. A high-protein keto diet may be a first step for a short time, before transitioning to another approach. Any of the recipes in this book can be adapted for this approach simply by leaving out the vegetables and fruits.

As I've said before, it is about experimenting and finding what works best for your body. You don't need to have the answer right away. I strongly urge you to keep a diary to write down what you eat every day and how you feel. If you like, you can follow through with accurate reporting from your healthcare professional with blood and hormone tests. Also remember that what works for your body may change as you get older, so flexibility is key.

FIVE MAIN APPROACHES TO GOING KETO

1 FULL KETOGENIC

Adopt a very low-carbohydrate lifestyle (20–50 grams of net carbs per day), so you are in a constant state of ketosis.

2 CYCLICAL KETOGENIC

Cycle in and out of ketosis.

Consume a higher level of carbohydrates (50–150 grams per day) 1–2 days per week, fortnight or month.

Consume less than 50 grams of net carbs on the other days.

Mimics the hunter–gatherer feast/famine cycle.

3 INTUITIVE KETOGENIC

Stay in a state of mild ketosis most of the time.

Fluctuate in and out of ketosis.

No need to count carbs but always stick to low-carb foods.

Tune in to your body and respond to how you feel.

4 TARGETED KETOGENIC

Eat all of your carbs either before or after training.

Geared towards athletes and fitness enthusiasts.

5 CARNIVORE KETOGENIC

Reduce carbs altogether, increase protein intake to 35–45% and reduce fat intake to 55–65%.

May help to reduce hunger and inflammation.

Possible first step before transitioning to another approach.

WHO IS THE KETO DIET SUITED TO?

The ketogenic diet is suitable for a wide range of people and has been shown to help men and women of all ages improve their health. However, it is important to note that it might not work for everyone. Babies, children, pregnant women and breastfeeding women have different needs, as they are growing their bodies or eating for two. It is recommended you always consult your healthcare professional when thinking of adopting a new eating regimen, especially if it involves fasting, you have blood-sugar issues, are on medication or have an existing medical condition.

EATING, FEASTING AND FASTING

For the many people who find that a cyclical ketogenic diet works for them, going keto is a cycle of eating, feasting and fasting. Eating the right foods to put your body into ketosis; occasionally feasting (and cycling out of ketosis) by having a high-carb day; and fasting intermittently.

EATING: WHAT TO EAT TO GO INTO KETOSIS

In order to go into ketosis, it is essential to reduce the amount of carbohydrates you eat so that your body is forced to start burning fat, instead of glucose, for fuel. The aim is to limit your net carb intake to below 50 grams per day (some people like to keep it closer to 20 grams per day).

I'm not one to count my carbs, but it is something you may like to do until you understand the quantities required. All the recipes in this book show the number of net carbs per serve, so that when you are starting out, you can easily calculate how many carbs you are consuming each day. Once you have a clearer idea about the level of carbohydrates in common foods, it will be easier to go by instinct as to how much of any particular food you should be eating. Remember that you should get most of your carbs from non-starchy veggies and generally eat them with fat and protein. See page 25 for a table showing the level of carbohydrates in common foods.

Once you start eating this way, and are consuming less than 50 grams of net carbs per day, it can take anywhere from 7 to 30 days for your body to go into ketosis. Everyone is different so don't panic if it takes a little while (and see page 22 for tips on how to know if you are in ketosis). During this early period of transition, you might feel some symptoms of the 'keto slump' – these should pass quickly, but see page 21 for some tips on helping to support your body during this time.

FEASTING: HOW TO CYCLE OUT OF KETOSIS

If you are trying a cyclical ketogenic approach, every week, fortnight, month or season, you will have a high-carb day (up to 150 grams of net carbs). It's simply a matter of experimenting with the timing and frequency of your high-carb days, listening to your body and seeing what feels best for you. I tend to fluctuate between 20 and 50 grams on most days, and then once in a while I up my carbs to 100–150 grams.

It's important to remember that on high-carb days, you should still be avoiding foods that are most likely to cause inflammation, such as dairy, grains, legumes and refined sugars. A high-carb day doesn't mean scoffing down potato chips, pizza, pasta, biscuits and other starchy foods that will simply convert to glucose and spike blood sugar levels. Instead, enjoy some healthy carbohydrate-rich options, such as sweet potato, pumpkin, parsnip, carrot, beetroot or keto bread. See the High-Carb Day chapter (page 148) for inspiration.

FASTING: A NATURAL PART OF THE KETO DIET

Fasting tends to be a natural part of the ketogenic diet, as once your body switches to fat-burning mode, you can often go for longer periods without feeling hungry.

If you do want to fast, I recommend easing into it. Start with intermittent fasting, which limits your eating time to a 6–8-hour period. For example, if you have your first meal of the day at 12 pm, your last meal will be before 8 pm. This means you are fasting for 16–18 hours between meals. For women, some nutritionists recommend fasting for only 14–15 hours, though there are also many women who thrive on 16–18 hours.

If you can, start with setting aside one day a week to fast intermittently. Eat your last meal before 6 pm in the evening and don't have your next meal until 10 am or 12 pm on the following day. Once you get into the swing of things, you can do this seven days a week. Depending on what I am doing, I often eat only one meal a day. Generally, my first meal of the day is around 2–4 pm, with perhaps a broth or celery juice in the morning. Sometimes I go 48 hours without eating and instead drink water and bone broth. On the other hand, when I am on a surfing holiday, I am very happy to eat three meals a day, as my body demands it. The key here is that I am flexible, listen to my body and adapt the food I eat accordingly.

It's important to note that fasting may not be the right option for you. Make sure you discuss it with your healthcare professional before you start, especially if you are have type 2 diabetes, hormonal imbalances, kidney disease or cancer. Fasting is not recommended for babies, children, teenagers, the elderly or pregnant or breastfeeding women.

MINDFUL EATING

I encourage you to get rid of distractions and commit to sitting down and slowly chewing your food without the interruption of your phone, work or anything else. For work lunches, change the environment and try to get 20 minutes outside; sit in a park with your shoes off and give yourself the gift of connecting with nature.

HONOUR YOUR FOOD SOURCE

I encourage you, wherever possible, to grow your own produce or choose local, organic veggies. Opt for pasture-raised or grass-fed meat and chicken, wild game and wild-caught seafood. We need to get behind farmers who honour our ecology and support food systems that take care of the health of our soil.

FIVE STEPS TO GET YOU STARTED ON A KETO DIET

 GET RID OF REFINED CARBS

The keto diet works best when you've removed refined sugar, grains and grain-based foods, such as pasta and bread, from your diet. Spend a few days, weeks or even months eliminating these before you transition to keto. Once you have removed these foods, you will already be well on your way. Your carbs will be coming from healthy sources, such as vegetables, nuts and seeds, and you can then play around with different levels of carbs, fat and protein to see what works best for your body.

 EMBRACE HEALTHY FATS

The idea is to replace carbohydrates with good-quality, healthy oils and fats. For cooking, I recommend coconut oil – which can withstand high temperatures – as well as lard, tallow and chicken and duck fat. I use olive, macadamia and avocado oils in salad dressings or to drizzle over meat, seafood and vegetables.

Healthy fats can also be found in organic grass-fed meat, pastured eggs, wild-caught seafood, avocados, nuts and seeds. Raw cacao butter is another excellent source of fat – I use it in baking and smoothies. I also love MCT (medium-chain triglycerides) oil, which contains a special type of saturated fatty acid that is easily digested to provide fast, sustained energy. Try adding it to smoothies and salad dressings. For more information on which fats to include when going keto, see pages 30–31.

 EAT ADEQUATE PROTEIN

Protein is an essential building block for the body and plays an important role in helping to regulate its processes. It is also important as it helps us to feel satiated for longer. I recommend getting about 25% of your daily energy from protein (with 70% from fat and 5% from carbs). However, as always, this can vary greatly from person to person, so it's important to pay attention to your body and see what works.

I choose the fattiest cuts of meat and seafood instead of the low-fat cuts or animals with lean protein. They are cheaper and more flavoursome, and it's also a great way to increase your fat intake to help your body go into ketosis.

 STAY HYDRATED

Staying hydrated is key when you are going keto. Water is also a natural appetite suppressant and hydration promotes weight loss. Headaches, muscle cramps and weakness occur if there is an electrolyte imbalance, so adjusting your salt intake can help your body cope and adjust. I recommend drinking 1–2 cups of bone broth a day and including good-quality unrefined sea salt or Himalayan salt in your diet, to boost vitality as you experience ketosis.

5 TOP UP ON KEY MINERALS

As you transition to a keto diet, it's important to ensure that you are getting enough key minerals, such as iodine and magnesium. These help to boost energy and also play a supportive role in the hormonal, digestive and neurological systems. I like to include sea vegetables such as seaweed in my diet to make sure I am getting enough iodine. Magnesium is present in avocado, nuts and seeds and oily fish, but my favourite way to make sure I am getting enough is to add magnesium flakes to the bath, as it gets absorbed easily through the skin.

KETO FOOD PYRAMID

NUTS, SEEDS & LOW-CARB FRUITS

BONE BROTH & FERMENTED VEGETABLES & DRINKS

NIGHTSHADES AND LOW-CARB VEGETABLES

VERY LOW-CARB VEGETABLES

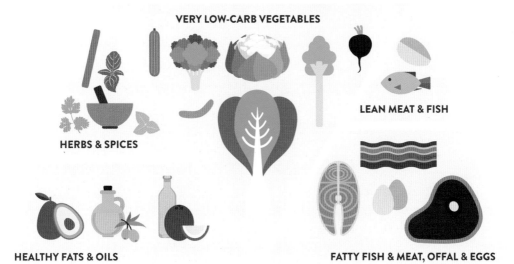

LEAN MEAT & FISH

HERBS & SPICES

HEALTHY FATS & OILS

FATTY FISH & MEAT, OFFAL & EGGS

AVOIDING THE KETO SLUMP

When you go keto you are rewiring your metabolism to run on a different type of fuel. For both the body and mind, it can take a bit of getting used to. That's why it's important to do whatever is needed to support yourself on your health journey. Listen to your body and remember that any change to your existing diet can result in a slump, so always make sure you have plenty of support and adequate rest.

WHAT IS THE KETO SLUMP?

The first 3–4 weeks (and sometimes longer, depending on your current state of health) are always the toughest. Generally, during this time, people experience what is known as keto flu. It can occur as the body switches from short, sharp sugar burning to slow, sustained fat burning. The symptoms include headaches, thick brain fog, exhaustion, constipation, diarrhoea, dizziness and irritability. Often, in the early stages of adapting to ketosis, these are the results of not eating, hydrating or resting enough. To help prevent this happening, here are some easy steps to take.

GET LOTS OF HYDRATION

Drink the purest filtered water possible – around 2 litres a day is good, but listen to your body.

INCLUDE ELECTROLYTES, ESPECIALLY SODIUM, MAGNESIUM AND POTASSIUM

You may wish to increase your salt intake to 2 teaspoons of unrefined sea or Himalayan salt, and include 300–400 milligrams of magnesium and 1–2 grams of potassium each day for a period of time. Going keto really flushes out water weight, and tons of electrolytes leave with it.

MOVE GENTLY EVERY DAY

Walk, swim, cycle, dance, practise yoga or just take the dog out. Whatever type of low-level, gentle exercise you love will be perfectly paired to going keto.

ENJOY SOME LOW-CARB VEGETABLES AND FRUIT

Raspberries, blackberries, strawberries and blueberries are all quite low in sugar and extremely high in phytonutrients.

GET AS MUCH REST AND SLEEP AS YOU NEED

Perhaps look at mind-calming techniques such as breathing and meditation, and avoid spending too much time in front of electronic devices. I also love using cold water therapy to boost my energy – if you are interested, you can start by simply having a cold shower every day.

TESTING FOR KETONES

Testing for ketone bodies can help you understand what happens in your body when you change the type and amount of food you eat, when you eat and the exercise you do. And it can help you understand your ideal ketone levels. Here are the three main testing methods.

URINE TESTS

Kits are available from pharmacies and are cheap and easy to use. However, they are not as accurate as blood tests. While urine tests can tell you when you are transitioning into ketosis, they do not always work effectively once you have been in ketosis for a longer time.

BLOOD TESTS

This is the most accurate – but expensive – way to test. You can buy a blood ketone meter and ketone test strips, then do a finger-prick test to see definitively if you are in ketosis.

BREATH TESTS

This is the newest form of testing. You can buy a keto breath tester online; however, the readings aren't very specific and there isn't much research on the reliability of this method.

USING YOUR SYMPTOMS TO KNOW WHEN YOU'RE IN KETOSIS

If you don't have any testing equipment, these are the signs that indicate you are in ketosis.

MENTAL CLARITY AND FOCUS DRAMATICALLY IMPROVE

Think about it – when you eat carbs, there are energy swings, which lead to mental performance swings. This does not happen when you are in a state of ketosis. Some people experience a feeling of euphoria once in ketosis.

CRAVINGS DISAPPEAR AND HUNGER IS CONTROLLED

When fat is burned as fuel, your body has a constant ready supply of energy. The healthy fats in your diet also help you feel full for longer.

LONG-LASTING ENERGY

It takes about 90 minutes for your body to use up the energy from eating carbs and then you start to 'crash'. This doesn't happen when you're in ketosis because your body is running off an almost limitless source of fuel.

FEELING THIRSTY AND EXPERIENCING A METALLIC TASTE IN THE MOUTH

When you're adapting to a keto diet, your body uses up excess glycogen and increases urination. If you're not adding in some salt or electrolytes you'll probably be pretty thirsty. You may also experience a metallic taste in your mouth.

CARBS IN COMMON FOODS AND DRINKS

CARBS IN COMMON FOODS

When you first start following a ketogenic diet, you may find it helpful to measure your net carbohydrate intake. The table opposite outlines the carbohydrates found in some of the common foods you'll cook and eat when going keto.

NET CARBS VS TOTAL CARBS

A common mistake people make when going keto is counting the total carbs in foods instead of the net carbs. This can lead to a restriction of foods high in dietary fibre. The reason we subtract the fibre from the total carb count is because fibre is an indigestible carbohydrate. It isn't absorbed into our system and doesn't affect our blood sugar. To figure out the net carbs, simply subtract the fibre from the total carbs. For example, 100 grams of almonds contains 22 grams of total carbs and 12 grams of fibre, so the net carb count is 10 grams.

TOTAL CARB COUNT – FIBRE COUNT = NET CARBS

MACRONUTRIENTS AND COUNTING CARBS: RELAX AND LISTEN TO YOUR BODY

When it comes to ketogenic diets, you'll often hear people talking about macronutrients or 'macros', which refer to the three key nutrients that all food can be broken down into: fat, protein and carbohydrate. There are lots of different recommendations out there, but the standard ketogenic diet advocates obtaining roughly 70% of your energy from fat, 25% from protein and 5% from carbs.

All of the recipes in this book show macronutrient percentages, as some people find it helpful as a general guide when they are first starting out. However, I don't like to prescribe exact percentages that everyone should stick to – people's bodies are so different in the way they metabolise food and I think it's important to not get too obsessive over the exact macronutrient percentages. It may be more useful to look at your approximate macro breakdown for the whole day rather than getting too caught up in the macros of each individual meal.

The same applies to counting carbs. Yes, you may need to count carbs when you first start out to make sure that you are consuming roughly between 20 and 50 grams of net carbs when you want to be in ketosis. However, I don't think it's helpful to count them compulsively or get stressed about whether you've had 35 or 35.5 grams of carbohydrates that day. Remember that all of the figures in the table opposite are estimations only – the exact amount of carbohydrates in ingredients can vary depending on where they are grown, whether they are in season and how you cook them.

So try to relax and listen to your body – keep a journal about what you have eaten and how you have felt, and try a more intuitive approach. Once you have been on a ketogenic diet for a while you will begin to understand when your body is in ketosis by the way you feel. You'll have more energy, feel clear-headed and you won't feel hungry between meals. This is the best way to figure out if you're consuming the right carb, fat and protein ratios for your own unique body. And as long as you are cooking with nutrient-dense whole foods, including healthy fats and good-quality protein, and avoiding grains, legumes and dairy, you can't go too far wrong!

Food/Drink	Net Carbohydrates	Food/Drink	Net Carbohydrates
Almonds (28 g)	3	Kombucha (250 ml)	7
Apple (100 g)	11	Liver (chicken) (100 g)	1
Artichokes (100 g)	1	Macadamia nuts (28 g)	2
Avocado (1 medium)	5	Meat (chicken, beef, pork) (100 g)	0
Banana (100 g)	20	Mussels (100 g)	7
Blackberries (100 g)	5	Okra (100 g)	4
Blueberries (100 g)	12	Olives (28 g)	1
Bok choy (100 g)	1	Onion (100 g)	8
Brazil nuts (28 g)	1	Orange (100 g)	9
Broccoli (100 g)	4	Oysters (100 g)	5
Brussels sprouts (100 g)	5	Parsnip (100 g)	13
Cabbage (100 g)	4	Pecans (28 g)	1
Capsicum (100 g)	4	Pistachios (28 g)	4
Carrots (100 g)	7	Pumpkin (100 g)	6
Cashews (28 g)	8	Pumpkin seeds (28 g)	3
Cauliflower (100 g)	3	Radish (100 g)	2
Celery (100 g)	2	Raspberries (100 g)	6
Chia seeds (28 g)	2	Rocket (100 g)	2
Clams (100 g)	4	Sesame seeds (28 g)	0
Coconut flour (28 g)	6	Silverbeet (100 g)	3
Coconut water (250 ml)	7	Spinach, raw (100 g)	1
Cucumber (100 g)	3	Strawberries (100 g)	5
Dates (100 g)	71	Sunflower seeds (28 g)	4
Egg (1 large)	<1	Sweet potato (100 g)	17
Fennel (100 g)	4	Tomatoes (100 g)	3
Fish (100 g)	0	Unsweetened cacao powder (28 g)	6
Flaxseeds (28 g)	1	Walnuts (28 g)	1
Kale (100 g)	6	Zucchini (100 g)	2

10 TIPS FOR CREATING YOUR KETO KITCHEN

 SPRING CLEAN YOUR CUPBOARDS, FRIDGE AND FREEZER

Be brutal! Get rid of all processed, highly refined carbohydrates and sugar-filled foods, vegetable and seed oils and margarine spreads. This means ditching anything that contains gluten, grains, dairy, soy, legumes or refined sugar, and will include everything from ready-made sauces to refined white flour, rice, bread and pasta. These ingredients won't help you on your keto journey. It's also an opportunity to wipe down the shelves and surrounding area so the physical space is clean and ready to be restocked with the good stuff. If you can't stand throwing food out, donate to your local food bank.

 TRACK DOWN SOME LOCAL SUPPLIERS

Have fun and start exploring ways you can get your hands on all the healthy ingredients you'll need. I recommend you shop around for fresh organic ingredients and support those in your community who are growing, farming and harvesting food sustainably. If you can, buy your meat and veggies from farmers' markets, organic and health-food stores, or from the organic section of your supermarket.

 SHOP MINDFULLY FOR YOUR PANTRY STAPLES

The first rule of thumb is to always read labels! This is *the* best way to understand exactly what's in your food. Buying pantry staples in bulk from your local organic or bulk-food store is a clever way to save on cost. It's also well worth checking out online shopping options that deliver direct to your door; this helps keep you on track when you are busy.

 BUY FRESH AS OFTEN AS POSSIBLE

Shopping for fresh, unprocessed foods that are as close as possible to their natural state is the essence of keto. Aim to shop a few times a week and strike up relationships with the people you buy from. It makes the whole experience more enjoyable. You'll learn from your greengrocer what's best and in season and your butcher can advise on top cuts of beef, poultry and wild game. Source a few bones every few weeks to boil up a nutritious bone broth. And don't forget your fishmonger for wild-caught, sustainable fish and seafood.

Shopping on a budget and can't afford to buy all organic? Learn which fruits and veggies are on the Dirty Dozen and the Clean Fifteen lists, which can be found online and detail the vegetables and fruits that have the most and least pesticide residue respectively. This way, you'll know what to avoid and what to spend your money on.

5 STOCK THE FREEZER FOR EMERGENCIES

I encourage you to see food as medicine. Embrace making your meals from scratch and carry packed meals with you when you travel. Modern life is busy, so to keep on track, a well-stocked freezer is essential. I make and freeze bone broths and soups as go-to staples. I'm also a big fan of making extra so there are leftovers to pop in the freezer (and thaw on those nights when we need a fast meal). And freezing avocados and berries means you've always got them on hand to create tasty, refined-sugar-free treats.

6 ADD CULTURE TO YOUR KITCHEN

Make your own cultured vegetables – such as sauerkraut and kimchi – every few weeks. It is cheaper than buying ready-made fermented veggies and you can play around with flavours. Also try your hand at making kombucha and dairy-free kefir.

7 MAKE YOUR OWN SPROUTS

I really enjoy growing my own broccoli and radish sprouts in sprouting jars. They are inexpensive to make and are one of the best superfoods you'll ever try. I put sprouts on everything and sometimes add a simple dressing.

8 GROW YOUR OWN PRODUCE

Grow as much as you can: herbs, fruit, veggies. Keep chickens, if you can, to supply you with the freshest eggs. The simple act of growing your own food brings a new-found respect and connection to the earth.

9 DRINK THE PUREST WATER

I am a firm believer that the purest water is key to optimal health. I actually recommend you sort out your water situation before you change your diet. I make sure I have the freshest and cleanest possible water available at all times, and when I leave the house I always take 1–2 litres with me. I personally avoid any water that has fluoride or chlorine in it.

10 GET YOUR BROTH ON

Every week in our house we make a big batch of broth to drink straight up or to use in soups and braises. Use the cleanest water and best quality bones available and embrace this once very popular life skill.

THE KETO PANTRY

PANTRY	
Apple cider vinegar (raw)	Oils (coconut, extra-virgin olive, avocado, MCT)
Cacao butter	Salt (unrefined varieties, such as sea, Himalayan)
Cacao powder (raw and unsweetened)	Seaweed (dulse, nori* and other seaweed)
Coconut flour	Seed crackers
Coconut milk/cream	Seeds (chia, pumpkin, sunflower, sesame)
Coconut, shredded	Spices (turmeric, black pepper, paprika, cumin)
Collagen powder (grass fed and marine)	Sprout seeds (broccoli, radish)
Dried herbs	Supplements (iodine, magnesium)
Fire tonic (medicinally spiced apple cider vinegar drink)	Sweeteners* (liquid stevia, monk fruit sweetener, xylitol, erythritol, honey)
Fish sauce	Tahini
Gelatine powder* (grass fed)	Tamari/coconut aminos
Lemons and limes	Tapioca flour*
Nut and seed flours (such as almond meal)	Tomatoes (jarred)
Nuts (almonds, macadamias, pecans, walnuts)	Vanilla (beans, paste, powder)

FRIDGE	
Bacon, ham and salami (free range and nitrate free)	Dressings, homemade
Coconut yoghurt (page 196)	Eggs (organic and free range)
Curry pastes	Fermented drinks (kombucha, dairy-free kefir)

FRIDGE	
Fermented vegetables (sauerkraut, kimchi) (page 197)	Nut and seed butters
Fish and shellfish	Nut cheeses (page 203)
Ghee (if choosing to include dairy)	Nut milks (my favourites are coconut, cashew and almond) and hemp milk
Good-quality animal fat* (lard, tallow, duck fat)	Offal
Herbs (basil, parsley, mint, coriander)	Olives
Kelp noodles and other sea vegetables	Pâté (page 70)
Keto bread (page 200)	Pickles
Low-carb fruits (blueberries, raspberries, blackberries, strawberries)	Salmon roe/caviar
Low-carb vegetables (cucumbers, celery, lettuce, tomatoes, silverbeet, cabbage, spring onions, radishes, cauliflower, broccoli)	Sprouts
Mayonnaise, homemade (page 201)	Sriracha chilli sauce, homemade (page 203)
Meats (all varieties, fattier cuts)	Tomato ketchup, homemade (page 204)

FREEZER	
Avocados (diced, for adding to smoothies and treats)	Bones for making broth
Bananas (chopped, for adding to smoothies on high-carb days)	Keto bread, sliced (page 200)
Berries (blueberries, raspberries, blackberries, strawberries)	Leftovers – to ensure you always have something healthy to hand when you need to eat
Bone broth (beef, chicken, fish) (pages 193, 195 and 198)	Lemon and lime juice (frozen in ice-cube trays)

* See Glossary for more information on these ingredients

LOVE YOUR FATS!

CHICKEN FAT

DUCK FAT

MELTED LARD (PIG FAT)

EXTRA-VIRGIN OLIVE OIL

MELTED DUCK FAT

SUET (RAW BEEF FAT)

MELTED TALLOW (RENDERED BEEF FAT)

As well as providing us with energy and keeping us feeling full for longer, healthy fats supply us with vitamins A, D, E and K, and support the health of our nervous, immune and digestive systems. Here are some of my favourite sources of fat. The animal fats and coconut oil are great for cooking, as they have high smoke points, while extra-virgin olive oil is wonderful in dressings and drizzled over dishes. Other favourite sources are avocados, eggs and macadamia nuts and oil.

COCONUT OIL

TALLOW (RENDERED BEEF FAT)

MELTED CHICKEN FAT

LARD (PIG FAT)

KETO-FRIENDLY FOOD SWAPS

Building a keto pantry starts with knowing where your food comes from and what's in it, so always read the labels and try to choose the most natural ingredients possible. By making some simple swaps, you can have a pantry, fridge and freezer that nurtures your health. Here are some of my favourite keto-friendly foods to use instead of less healthy alternatives.

- Large field or portobello mushrooms, lettuce or cabbage leaves instead of grain-based rolls and burger buns

- Lettuce, kale, cabbage, silverbeet leaves or cauliflower wraps instead of tacos and tortillas

- Spiralised vegetables (try zucchini, carrot and pumpkin) or kelp noodles instead of grain-based pasta and noodles

- Mashed cauliflower or parsnip (pages 194 and 202), or cauliflower or broccoli rice (page 194) instead of potatoes, pasta and rice

- Almond meal or coconut flour instead of wheat flour

- Keto bread (page 200) instead of grain-based breads

- Coconut milk or cream, hemp or nut milks instead of dairy milk

- Coconut aminos, fish sauce or tamari instead of soy sauce

- Cauliflower pizza bases instead of wheat-flour pizza bases

- Sushi made with cauliflower or broccoli rice instead of rice

- Flaxseed and chia seed crackers with nut or pumpkin cheese (page 203) instead of crackers and cheese

- Zucchini or parsnip fries instead of French fries

- Kale chips or a handful of nuts and seeds instead of potato chips and processed snacks

- Kombucha, dairy-free kefir, apple cider vinegar drinks or coconut water instead of soft drinks and energy drinks

- Herbal tea instead of a glass of wine

- Turmeric nut milk latte instead of coffee

BREA

KFAST

I love to start the day with a couple of glasses of water. A lot of people mistake hunger for thirst, and that is why drinking water upon rising in the morning is a great way to start your day. I like to add lemon zest, juice and pulp or a splash of apple cider vinegar. Fire tonic (a medicinally spiced apple cider vinegar drink that has a bit of kick to it) is fantastic, too, or you could add a probiotic elixir, such as the liquid from kraut or kimchi. Have a play and mix up your water with these additions and see how your body responds to this change in your morning routine.

SIMPLE LEMON WATER

SERVES 1–2

1 litre filtered water, at room temperature
 or lukewarm
juice of 1 lemon or 2 tablespoons apple
 cider vinegar

Stir the water and lemon juice or vinegar together and drink, on an empty stomach, in the first 30 minutes upon waking. Food or other drinks should not be consumed for at least 30–60 minutes afterwards.

Per Serve: Total carbs: 2 g | Net carbs: 2 g | Fat: 0 g | Protein: 0 g

Beef bone broth is what I call a superfood! It contains so many nutrients our bodies can utilise and thrive on. Delicious, comforting and cheap to make, bone broth should become a regular feature in your cooking repertoire. I recommend making 5–10 litres of broth every couple of weeks and freezing it in portions so you always have a ready supply on hand. My children love to have a cup of broth – or beef tea as we call it – in the mornings with their breakfast before heading off to school. This broth forms the base for so many wonderful soups, curries, stews and braised dishes, and you can also pop it in smoothies and popsicles (page 175).

BEEF TEA

SERVES 1

300 ml Beef Bone Broth (page 193)
1–2 pinches of sea salt
½ teaspoon lemon juice or apple cider vinegar,
    or to taste (optional)

Heat the broth in a saucepan until just simmering and stir through the salt to taste. Add some lemon juice or vinegar, if desired. Pour the hot broth into a mug and serve.

NOTE
If your broth has been skimmed of all fat, when making the tea, stir in ½–1 teaspoon of coconut oil or good-quality animal fat.

VARIATION
You may like to substitute Chicken Bone Broth (page 195) for the beef bone broth.

Per Serve: Total carbs: 1 g | Net carbs: 1 g | Fat: 0 g | Protein: 6 g

If you love smoothies as part of your diet, why not make your own gut-healthy, keto-friendly version that is low in sugar, full of good fats and will sustain you throughout the morning? Collagen powders and blends, available online or at health-food stores, help with gut repair, sustain skin, nail and hair health and promote general wellbeing. Please don't fall into the trap of buying high-sugar whey or pea protein powders – they will not do your body or mind any favours.

CHOC–BLUEBERRY SMOOTHIE WITH COLLAGEN

SERVES 1–2

400 ml coconut milk or milk of choice (non dairy)
80 g (½ cup) fresh or frozen blueberries
½ banana, roughly chopped
3 tablespoons collagen
1 tablespoon raw cacao
½ avocado
sweetener of your choice (liquid stevia*, xylitol*, monk fruit sweetener*, honey), to taste (optional)
1–2 pinches of ground cinnamon
45 g (⅓ cup) ice cubes

* See Glossary

Place all the ingredients in a high-speed blender and blend until smooth. Pour into glasses and serve.

VARIATION

HOT CHOCOLATE WITH COLLAGEN

SERVES 1

300 ml coconut milk (you can also use almond, macadamia or hemp milk)
1–2 tablespoons chocolate collagen blend
sweetener of your choice (liquid stevia*, xylitol*, monk fruit sweetener*, honey), to taste (optional)

* See Glossary

Pour the milk into a small saucepan. Stir through the collagen blend to combine. Heat over medium–low heat, stirring occasionally, until heated through. Pour into a mug, sip and enjoy!

You have to love the person who invented the humble muffin tray and helped make the lives of parents everywhere that little bit easier. We use our muffin tray a lot, and make all different kinds of goodies in them, from savoury egg or meat muffins to keto treats.

These classic sausage and egg muffins can be made in bulk and are super affordable. Changing things up with your muffin ingredients is also easy: try replacing the sausage with chicken, bacon, fish or prawns, add whatever low-carb vegetables you feel like, then pop them in the oven and minutes later you will have a few days of speedy keto breakfasts or work or school lunches sorted.

SAUSAGE, EGG AND SPINACH MUFFINS

MAKES 12

2 tablespoons coconut oil or
    good-quality animal fat*,
    plus extra for greasing
½ onion, finely chopped
2 garlic cloves, finely chopped
8 eggs
50 g baby spinach leaves, chopped
4 sausages (about 300 g),
    cut into bite-sized pieces
sea salt and freshly ground
    black pepper
Tomato Ketchup (page 204),
    to serve

* See Glossary

Preheat the oven to 180°C (160°C fan-forced). Grease a 12-hole standard muffin tray.

Heat the coconut oil or fat in a frying pan over medium heat. Add the onion and sauté for about 5 minutes, or until softened. Add the garlic and cook for a further minute. Remove from the heat and allow to cool.

Crack the eggs into a large bowl and whisk until smooth. Add the onion, garlic, spinach and sausage and mix until well combined. Season with salt and pepper.

Spoon the egg mixture evenly into the prepared tray until level with the rim. Bake for 15–20 minutes until the muffins have risen and a skewer inserted in the centre of one comes out clean. Allow to cool in the tray for 2 minutes before turning out onto a wire rack to cool completely.

Serve with tomato ketchup. The muffins can be stored in an airtight container in the fridge for up to 5 days.

Per Serve: Total carbs: 7 g | Net carbs: 6 g | Fat: 35 g | Protein: 26 g | Fat 70% | Protein 24% | Carbs 6%

I was first introduced to this dish in a café in New Zealand, and have since learned that it's a bit of a national treasure. I can see why! On a cold day, it doesn't disappoint. If you want to keep your carb intake super low, ditch the bread.

MINCE ON TOAST WITH POACHED EGG AND SPINACH

SERVES 4

2 tablespoons apple cider vinegar
4 eggs
2 teaspoons coconut oil or good-quality animal fat*
2 garlic cloves, finely chopped
1 bunch of English spinach (about 200 g), stems removed and leaves torn in half
4 slices of Keto Bread (page 200), toasted
chilli flakes, to serve
parsley sprigs, to serve

Mince
2 tablespoons coconut oil or good-quality animal fat
1 onion, finely chopped
1 carrot, finely chopped
1 celery stalk, finely chopped
3 garlic cloves, finely chopped
700 g beef mince
3 tablespoons tomato paste
1 tablespoon tamari
3 tablespoons red wine (such as shiraz)
500 ml (2 cups) Beef or Chicken Bone Broth (page 193 or 195)
1 teaspoon thyme leaves, chopped
sea salt and freshly ground black pepper
chilli flakes, to taste (optional)

* See Glossary

To make the mince, heat the coconut oil or fat in a large frying pan over medium heat. Add the onion, carrot and celery and cook, stirring occasionally, for 5 minutes, or until the onion has softened. Stir in the garlic and cook for 30 seconds, or until fragrant. Next, add the mince and cook, using a wooden spoon to break up any large chunks, for 8 minutes, or until brown. Stir in the tomato paste and tamari and cook for 2 minutes. Pour in the wine, bring to the boil and cook until reduced by half. Add the broth and thyme, stir well and bring to a simmer. Reduce the heat to low and cook for 30 minutes, or until most of the liquid has evaporated. Season with salt and pepper and the chilli flakes (if using).

Meanwhile, when just about ready to serve, poach the eggs. Pour the vinegar into a saucepan of boiling salted water. Reduce the heat to medium–low so the water is just simmering. Crack an egg into a cup and, using a wooden spoon, stir the simmering water in one direction to form a whirlpool, then drop the egg into the centre. Repeat with the remaining eggs and cook for 3 minutes, or until the eggs are cooked to your liking. Use a slotted spoon to remove the eggs, then drain on paper towel.

Heat the coconut oil or fat in a large non-stick frying pan over medium–high heat. Add the garlic and sauté for 10 seconds, or until fragrant. Add the spinach and sauté for about 1 minute, or until the spinach is just wilted. Season with salt and pepper.

Divide the toast among warm serving plates, then top each with the wilted spinach, mince and a poached egg. Sprinkle on some pepper, chilli flakes and parsley and serve.

Per Serve: Total carbs: 16 g | Net carbs: 12 g | Fat: 67 g | **Protein:** 54 g | Fat 68% | Protein 24% | Carbs 8%

This is the quintessential keto recipe, in my book (pardon the pun!). It ticks all the boxes from both a nutritional and flavour point of view. A dish like this should see you through a large portion of your day, with a good amount of healthy fat and protein from the fish, egg and avocado. Feel free to have a play with the veggies, depending on what is in season, and change up the protein to suit your own tastes.

SIMPLE SALMON AND EGG BOWL

SERVES 4

1 large handful of red vein sorrel or
    mixed salad leaves
1 handful of coriander leaves
1 tablespoon extra-virgin olive oil
2 teaspoons lime juice
sea salt and freshly ground
    black pepper
4 eggs
2 teaspoons fish sauce
1 tablespoon sesame oil
4 x 150 g salmon fillets, skin off
3 tablespoons coconut oil or
    good-quality animal fat*
juice of ½ lemon
2 radishes, thinly sliced
1 handful of alfalfa sprouts
4 tablespoons pink sauerkraut
1 avocado, cubed
2 teaspoons toasted sesame seeds

* See Glossary

Combine the sorrel or salad leaves and coriander in a bowl, add the olive oil and lime juice and toss lightly to coat. Season with salt and pepper to taste. Set aside.

Whisk the eggs, fish sauce and sesame oil in a bowl until combined. Set aside.

Season the salmon fillets with salt and pepper.

Heat 2 tablespoons of the coconut oil or fat in a non-stick frying pan over high heat. Add the salmon to the pan and fry for 1 minute on each side or until crispy and golden. Remove from the pan and squeeze over the lemon juice.

In the same pan, heat the remaining coconut oil or fat over medium heat. Pour in the egg mixture and cook for 1 minute, stirring gently by lifting and pushing the mixture from the outside to the centre with a wooden spoon. Remove from the heat and gently fold the mixture a few times. Allow the eggs to stand for 30–60 seconds so that the residual heat finishes the cooking.

Divide the eggs and salmon among four serving bowls, then add the dressed salad leaves, radish, sprouts, sauerkraut and avocado. Sprinkle over the sesame seeds and serve immediately.

Per Serve: Total carbs: 11 g | Net carbs: 5 g | Fat: 47 g | Protein: 48 g | Fat 65% | Protein 30% | Carbs 5%

This may seem like a strange pairing, but you have to trust me and give it a try. I was fortunate enough to visit Mexico recently, where I tried this soup. It was a revelation. With each mouthful the nourishing, lightly spiced broth became more and more addictive, each slurp better than the last. To make this a larger meal, try adding a soft-boiled egg or, to thicken, whisk in a raw egg at the end of cooking. This is awesome not only for breakfast, but for a light lunch and dinner too.

MEXICAN CHICKEN BROTH WITH AVOCADO

SERVES 1

350 ml Chicken Bone Broth
   (page 195)
45 g (¼ cup) leftover cooked finely-
   shredded chicken (optional)
sea salt and freshly ground
   black pepper
¼ avocado, sliced lengthways
¼ teaspoon Mexican spice mix
   (or more to taste)

To serve
coriander sprigs
sliced spring onion
lime cheeks
extra-virgin olive oil

Heat the broth and chicken (if using) in a small saucepan until simmering. Season with a pinch of salt and pepper.

Pour the broth into a bowl, then add the avocado and sprinkle on the Mexican spice mix. Scatter over some coriander sprigs and spring onion, drizzle with a little olive oil and squeeze some lime juice over the top. Stir, season and enjoy.

Leeks are enjoying a huge surge in popularity in the health world, as they are one of the most nutritious prebiotics nature has to offer. (Prebiotics are the fuel that good gut bacteria need to proliferate and stay healthy.) They are also a darling in the culinary world because of their amazing taste and versatility. When roasted, leeks become juicy, sweet and earthy, and when combined with good-quality fats, they soak up the deliciousness of the fats. Go ahead and experiment with your egg bake: try adding wild-caught salmon, sardines, sausages or olives, and serve with a salad and some kraut on the side.

LEEK, BROCCOLI AND EGG BAKE WITH BACON VINAIGRETTE

SERVES 6–8

2 tablespoons coconut oil or
   good-quality animal fat*,
   plus extra for greasing
1 onion, finely chopped
3 garlic cloves, finely chopped
6 eggs
150 ml coconut cream
250 ml (1 cup) Chicken Bone Broth
   (page 195)
pinch of freshly grated nutmeg
sea salt and freshly ground
   black pepper
2 leeks, white part only, halved
   lengthways and cut into
   4 cm lengths
1 head of broccoli (about 300 g),
   broken into florets
2 teaspoons finely snipped chives
½ teaspoon chilli flakes (optional)

Bacon vinaigrette

1 teaspoon coconut oil or
   good-quality animal fat
150 g rindless bacon rashers,
   finely diced
1 teaspoon lemon juice
1 teaspoon Dijon mustard
3 tablespoons olive oil

* See Glossary

Preheat the oven to 200°C (180°C fan-forced). Lightly grease a deep baking dish with coconut oil or fat.

Heat the coconut oil or fat in a frying pan over medium heat. Add the onion and cook, stirring occasionally, for 5 minutes, or until translucent. Add the garlic and cook for 30 seconds, or until fragrant. Remove from the heat and allow to cool.

Crack the eggs into a bowl, add the coconut cream, broth and nutmeg and whisk to combine. Season with salt and pepper.

Arrange the leek, broccoli and cooked onion and garlic in the prepared dish, then pour over the egg mixture. Bake for 40 minutes, or until the egg is set in the middle and golden on top.

To make the vinaigrette, heat the coconut oil or fat in a frying pan over medium heat. Add the bacon and fry, stirring occasionally, for 6–8 minutes until crispy and golden. Add the lemon juice and set aside to cool. Transfer to a bowl, then whisk in the mustard and olive oil and season with salt and pepper.

To serve, drizzle the vinaigrette over the egg bake and sprinkle on the chives and chilli flakes (if using).

   Per Serve: Total carbs: 11 g | Net carbs: 9 g | Fat: 32 g | Protein: 18 g | Fat 72% | Protein 18% | Carbs 10%

I am going to put this out there – sausages are actually a health food! That said, I need to emphasise that there are great sausages and then there are bad sausages. Try making your own or purchase organic sausages made from healthy, pasture-raised animals. A good sausage should only contain protein and plenty of healthy animal fat (this makes them juicy, delicious and perfect for the keto diet) and maybe some spices, herbs, onion, garlic and, if you are really lucky, offal. And that should be it. Here, I've teamed Italian sausage with loads of greens. Add some kraut for probiotic goodness if you like.

ITALIAN SAUSAGE WITH SAUTÉED GREENS

SERVES 6

1 kg Italian sausage, not linked if
    possible (ask your butcher)
3 tablespoons melted coconut oil or
    good-quality animal fat*
1½ bunches of broccolini
    (about 250 g)
1 bunch of cavolo nero (about 300 g),
    stems discarded and leaves torn
    into large pieces
sea salt and freshly ground
    black pepper

Almond dressing

80 ml (⅓ cup) extra-virgin olive oil
60 g almonds (activated if possible*),
    toasted and chopped
2 tablespoons apple cider vinegar or
    lemon juice
1 teaspoon Dijon mustard
2 tablespoons salted baby capers,
    rinsed well and patted dry

* See Glossary

Preheat the barbecue grill to medium–hot.

Combine all the dressing ingredients in a bowl with some salt and pepper and mix well. Set aside until needed.

Roll the sausage into a tight round, then insert a metal skewer through the sausage from one side to the other. Turn the sausage and insert another skewer to form a cross. This secures the sausage and makes it easy to turn when cooking. Brush both sides of the sausage with 1 tablespoon of the coconut oil or fat.

Cook the sausage, turning over every 2–3 minutes, for 10–12 minutes until golden brown and cooked through. Transfer to a board or platter.

Meanwhile, combine the broccolini and cavolo nero in a bowl, add the remaining coconut oil or fat and toss until well coated.

Heat a large frying pan over medium heat or the barbecue hotplate to medium. Add the broccolini and cavolo nero and sauté for 2 minutes. Pour 3 tablespoons of water over the greens, toss and cook for a further 2–3 minutes until wilted and cooked through. Season with salt and pepper.

Transfer the sautéed greens to a serving dish, spoon over the dressing and serve with the sausage.

Per Serve: Total carbs: 8 g | Net carbs: 3 g | Fat: 79 g | Protein: 29 g | Fat 83% | Protein 14% | Carbs 3%

Okay, can I please have your attention? Going keto does not give you a free pass to eat bacon until the pigs come home. I love bacon, but I do not eat a lot of it and here's why. Most bacon comes from pigs raised in inhumane conditions in sow stalls. Range and pasture–raised pigs are a lot better, but they may be fed genetically modified grains. Also, a lot of bacon contains nitrates and preservatives that can lead to ill health. Always purchase great-quality, free-range bacon – by doing this you will increase demand for humanely-raised pigs and help to change the system. And if you do enjoy bacon and eggs often, try swapping the bacon for a minute steak or some prawns or sardines. You can also make your own bacon using pork belly.

BACON, TOMATO AND SPINACH OMELETTE

SERVES 4

1 tablespoon melted coconut oil or
    good-quality animal fat*, plus extra
    for greasing
½ onion, finely chopped
2 rindless bacon rashers, chopped
6 eggs
sea salt and freshly ground
    black pepper
½ bunch of English spinach (about
    100 g), stems removed and leaves
    roughly chopped
6 cherry tomatoes, halved
1 handful of rocket leaves

* See Glossary

Preheat the oven to 220°C (200°C fan-forced).

Heat the coconut oil or fat in a frying pan over medium–high heat. Add the onion and cook, stirring occasionally, for 5 minutes, or until translucent. Add the bacon and cook for a further 5 minutes, or until lightly golden. Remove from the heat and allow to cool.

Whisk the eggs with a pinch of salt and pepper in a bowl.

Grease an ovenproof frying pan with a little coconut oil or fat. Scatter over the spinach and cooked onion mixture in a single layer. Pour over the egg mixture, then arrange the cherry tomatoes on top and press down lightly. Cook the omelette over medium heat for 1 minute, then transfer to the oven for 8–10 minutes until the egg is lightly golden on top and cooked through. Allow the omelette to rest for a minute in the pan, then top with the rocket and serve.

To me and many other parents, mince is the most delicious and versatile meat, perfect for meatballs, bolognese, burgers and in this simple dish. Add spinach or broccoli to the pan with the egg if you like.

LEBANESE SPICED LAMB WITH BABA GHANOUSH

SERVES 4

1 tablespoon coconut oil or
   good-quality animal fat*
4 eggs
flat-leaf parsley and mint leaves
4 radishes, halved or quartered
chilli flakes (optional)
extra-virgin olive oil

Baba ghanoush

1 large eggplant (about 500 g)
1½ tablespoons olive oil
50 g hulled tahini
2 Garlic Confit cloves (page 199)
1 tablespoon lemon juice
½ teaspoon ground cumin
⅛ teaspoon chilli powder
sea salt and freshly ground
   black pepper

Lebanese spiced lamb

2 tablespoons coconut oil or
   good-quality animal fat*
1 onion, finely chopped
4 garlic cloves, finely chopped
800 g lamb mince
2 teaspoons ground cumin
2 teaspoons ground coriander
2 teaspoons sweet paprika
2 teaspoons dried mint
1½ teaspoons ground allspice
¼ teaspoon ground cinnamon
2 bay leaves
250 ml (1 cup) Beef or Chicken
   Bone Broth (page 193 or 195)
1 long red chilli, deseeded and finely
   chopped, plus extra to serve
3 tablespoons pine nuts, toasted

* See Glossary

To make the baba ghanoush, cook the eggplant for 8–10 minutes over an open flame on the stovetop or barbecue, turning frequently until the skin is charred and blistered and the flesh feels soft when pressed with tongs. Place the charred eggplant in a large bowl, cover tightly with plastic wrap and set aside to cool. Transfer the cooled eggplant to a colander to drain, then peel and discard the skin. Place the eggplant flesh in the bowl of a food processor, add the olive oil, tahini, garlic, lemon juice, cumin and chilli powder and process until smooth. Season with salt and pepper. If the baba ghanoush is too thick, add a little cold water.

To make the Lebanese spiced lamb, heat the coconut oil or fat in a large frying pan over medium–high heat. Add the onion and sauté for 5 minutes, or until softened. Add the garlic and cook for 1 minute. Stir in the lamb mince and cook, using a wooden spoon to break up any large chunks, for 10 minutes, or until the mince is brown. Reduce the heat to medium–low. Add the spices, bay leaves, broth and chilli and cook for a further 15–20 minutes until most of the liquid has evaporated. Mix through the pine nuts and set aside, keeping warm.

Heat the coconut oil or fat in another large frying pan over medium heat. Crack in the eggs and cook until the whites are set, about 2½ minutes. Season with salt and pepper.

To serve, divide the baba ghanoush among four serving plates, then top with an egg and some mince. Scatter over the herbs and radish, sprinkle on some chilli flakes (if using) and extra fresh chilli and drizzle over some olive oil.

Per Serve: Total carbs: 18 g | Net carbs: 11 g | Fat: 71 g | Protein: 46 g | Fat 72% | Protein 21% | Carbs 7%

SEA

FOOD

A perfectly cooked piece of fish is one of life's greatest pleasures. The key is to get the best-quality wild salmon you can find. More and more fishmongers in Australia are now stocking wild Alaskan or Canadian salmon. You need to decide for yourself if you are happy to eat something flown halfway around the world. We do from time to time enjoy this as a treat. Serve with a salad or cooked vegetables of your choice.

SIMPLE OVEN-BAKED SALMON

SERVES 4

4 x 160 g salmon fillets, skin on,
   pin-boned
2 tablespoons melted coconut oil or
   good-quality animal fat*
sea salt and freshly ground
   black pepper
lemon wedges, to serve

* See Glossary

Preheat the oven to 200°C (180°C fan-forced).

Heat a heavy-based ovenproof frying pan over high heat until very hot. Brush the fish with the coconut oil or fat, season with salt and pepper and cook, skin-side down, for 30–60 seconds or until crispy.

Transfer the pan to the oven and cook the salmon, still with the skin-side down, for 3 ½–4 minutes for medium–rare (or until cooked to your liking) and until the skin is golden and crisp.

Flip the salmon, skin-side up, onto a plate and allow to rest for 2–3 minutes, keeping warm. At this point the salmon will be perfectly cooked, slightly pink and moist in the middle. Serve with some lemon wedges for squeezing over.

Per Serve: Total carbs: 0 g | Net carbs: 0 g | Fat: 68 g | Protein: 127 g | Fat 54% | Protein 46% | Carbs 0%

Who doesn't love a good stir-fry? They're super quick to put together, taste amazing and you can take them in so many different directions. Whip up this simple and delicious prawn stir-fry in less than 10 minutes. Serve with cauliflower rice if desired and you'll have a wonderful keto-friendly meal.

PRAWN, GINGER AND BROCCOLI STIR-FRY

SERVES 4

3 tablespoons coconut oil or good-quality animal fat*

500 g raw prawns, shelled and deveined, tails left intact

5 cm piece of ginger, cut into matchsticks

1 tablespoon finely chopped lemongrass, pale part only

½ onion, sliced

8 spring onions, white part only, cut into 6 cm lengths (reserve the green part for other recipes)

300 g broccoli, broken into florets

4 garlic cloves, thinly sliced

1 long red chilli, thinly sliced

2 tablespoons tamari

2 tablespoons fish sauce

2 teaspoons coconut sugar, honey or monk fruit sweetener* (optional)

250 ml (1 cup) Chicken Bone Broth (page 195)

1½ tablespoons tapioca flour*, mixed with 1 tablespoon water

2 handfuls of water spinach or baby spinach leaves

1 handful of Thai basil leaves

* See Glossary

Heat 1 tablespoon of the coconut oil or fat in a wok or large frying pan over medium–high heat. Add the prawns, in batches, and cook for 30 seconds on each side. Remove from the pan and set aside until needed.

Wipe the wok or pan clean, add the remaining coconut oil or fat and place over medium–high heat. Add the ginger, lemongrass, onion, spring onion, broccoli, garlic and chilli and stir-fry for 3–4 minutes until fragrant and starting to colour slightly.

Mix in the tamari, fish sauce, sweetener (if using), broth and tapioca mixture and simmer for 1 minute, or until the sauce thickens. Add the prawns and mix through until they are just cooked. Remove from the heat, toss through the spinach and Thai basil leaves and serve.

Holy broccomole! Broccomole is basically guacamole with some raw or cooked broccoli folded through it, which makes for an awesome accompaniment to so many things . . . eggs – poached, fried or boiled – grilled, steamed, poached or roasted meats and seafood, seed crackers, raw fish wrapped in nori, paleo nachos . . . the list goes on. Here, I demonstrate how to get a dish on the table from start to finish in under 10 minutes. Mind you, I get the girls to make the broccomole for me, so all I have to do is cook the fish and add some kraut.

PAN-FRIED SNAPPER WITH BROCCOMOLE

SERVES 4

4 x 160 g snapper fillets, skin on
    or off, pin-boned
sea salt and freshly ground
    black pepper
1 teaspoon lemon thyme leaves,
    chopped
2 tablespoons coconut oil
100 g sauerkraut
1 large handful of watercress sprigs
4 lemon wedges, to serve

Broccomole
100 g broccoli, broken into florets
1 avocado, diced or mashed
⅛ red onion, finely chopped
1 garlic clove, finely chopped
1 tablespoon lime juice
½ teaspoon chilli flakes (optional)
1 tablespoon extra-virgin olive oil,
    plus extra for drizzling
1 tablespoon chopped
    coriander leaves

Season the snapper fillets with salt and pepper and sprinkle over the thyme.

Heat the coconut oil in a large heavy-based frying pan over high heat. Fry the fish, skin-side down and in batches if necessary, for 2½–3 minutes, or until crispy. Flip over and cook for 2 minutes, or until the fish is just cooked through. Rest for 2 minutes.

To make the broccomole, bring a saucepan of salted water to the boil. Add the broccoli and cook for 3 minutes, or until just tender. Drain, then plunge the broccoli into ice-cold water to stop the cooking process. When the broccoli is completely cold, drain again, shake off any excess water and chop into small pieces. Place the avocado, onion, garlic, lime juice, chilli flakes (if using), olive oil, coriander and broccoli in a serving bowl and mix well. Season with salt and pepper.

To serve, divide the fish among four plates. Add the broccomole, sauerkraut and watercress, and drizzle with a little extra olive oil. Serve with the lemon wedges.

Per Serve: Total carbs: 7 g | Net carbs: 3 g | Fat: 21 g | Protein: 35 g | Fat 52% | Protein 41% | Carbs 7%

Poke bowls, which originated in Hawaii, have become very popular in Australia and New Zealand, which can only be a good thing when it comes to looking for healthy food options. Making poke is super easy and, here, I show you how.

SALMON POKE BOWL

SERVES 4

200 g daikon, cut into matchsticks
180 g red cabbage, finely shredded
180 g savoy cabbage, finely shredded
1 avocado, sliced
1 Lebanese cucumber, thinly sliced
400 g sashimi-grade salmon,
    cut into 1 cm cubes
1 teaspoon shichimi togarashi*,
    or to taste (optional)
1 tablespoon Furikake Seasoning
    (page 198)
2 tablespoons salmon roe
80 g Japanese Mayonnaise
    (page 199)
1 handful of coriander leaves
baby shiso leaves or micro herbs
    of your choice (optional)

Dressing
3 tablespoons tamari
1 garlic clove, finely grated
1 teaspoon finely grated ginger
2 teaspoons yuzu juice* or lemon juice
1½ teaspoons Sriracha Chilli Sauce
    (page 203)
2 teaspoons toasted sesame oil
3 tablespoons olive oil or
    avocado oil

* See Glossary

Place all the dressing ingredients in a bowl and whisk to combine.

Divide the daikon and cabbage among four serving bowls, then top with the avocado, cucumber and salmon. Sprinkle over the shichimi togarashi (if using) and furikake, add the salmon roe and finish with the Japanese mayonnaise, coriander and micro herbs. Pour over the dressing and eat immediately.

Per Serve: Total carbs: 17 g | Net carbs: 9 g | Fat: 41 g | Protein: 28 g | Fat 68% | Protein 20% | Carbs 12%

Sometimes we simply need to throw something together that takes only 2–3 minutes from start to finish. And that is where a recipe like this comes into its own, as it is not only fast, but super easy and nutritious, too. Feel free to use any type of raw, smoked or cooked seafood or animal protein that you have on hand. My favourites include sardines, smoked mackerel, wild salmon, tuna, chicken, slow-cooked lamb or pork. Add any salad ingredients you have in the crisper – think lettuce, leafy greens, crunchy vegetables – and a wicked dressing. I like a mayonnaise-based dressing with some essential healthy fats. You might also like to add boiled eggs and kraut.

QUICK FISH AND MAYO SALAD

SERVES 4

300 g jarred tuna* in brine, drained
    (or use mackerel, sardines or wild
    salmon)
1 celery stalk, finely diced
2 tablespoons finely chopped flat-leaf
    parsley leaves
100 g Mayonnaise (page 201)
2 tablespoons lemon juice
2 tablespoons extra-virgin olive oil,
    plus extra to serve
sea salt and freshly ground
    black pepper
1 Lebanese cucumber, thinly sliced
    using a mandoline or peeler
4 radishes, thinly sliced with
    a mandoline or peeler
¼ red onion, thinly sliced with
    a mandoline or peeler
½ iceberg lettuce, cut into
    3 cm wedges
1 handful of red vein sorrel (optional)

* See Glossary

Place the fish in a bowl. Add the celery, parsley, mayonnaise, lemon juice and olive oil and mix to combine. Season with salt and pepper.

To serve, divide the fish mixture among four serving bowls, then add the cucumber, radish, onion and iceberg lettuce. Scatter over the sorrel (if using), drizzle over some extra olive oil and sprinkle with a little pepper to finish.

Snapper is one of my all-time favourite fish to cook. It's so versatile and all you need to do is add some lemon on the side and it's amazing. Quick to cook, snapper is a wonderful, sustainable wild-caught fish that you can get pretty much anywhere. The secret to crispy skin is to dry the fish with paper towel and liberally season the skin with salt. Here, I pair snapper with braised fennel for a delicious keto meal.

CRISPY-SKINNED SNAPPER WITH BRAISED FENNEL

SERVES 4

70 ml melted coconut oil or
    good-quality animal fat*
2 fennel bulbs, cut into 1 cm thick
    slices, fronds and thinly sliced
    green stalks reserved to serve
150 ml Fish or Chicken Bone Broth
    (page 198 or 195), or water,
    plus extra if needed
sea salt and freshly ground
    black pepper
4 x 160 g snapper fillets, skin on,
    pin-boned
1 tablespoon finely snipped chives

To serve
extra-virgin olive oil, for drizzling
Aioli (page 192)
lemon wedges

* See Glossary

Heat 2 tablespoons of the coconut oil or fat in a large frying pan over medium heat. Add the sliced fennel bulb and cook for 5 minutes, or until starting to colour. Pour in the broth or water, reduce the heat to medium–low, cover and cook for a further 5–6 minutes until the fennel is cooked through. Add a little more broth or water if needed. Season with salt and pepper and keep warm.

While the fennel is cooking, coat the snapper fillets with 1 tablespoon of the coconut oil or fat and season with salt and pepper.

Heat another large frying pan over medium–high heat and add the remaining coconut oil or fat. Add the fish, skin-side down, top with a sheet of baking paper and place a heavy-based pan on top. Cook for 2½–3 minutes until the skin is golden and crisp. Flip the fish over and cook for a further minute, or until the fish is just cooked through. Remove the fish from the pan, place on a plate and allow to rest.

Place the fennel on a platter, then scatter over the fennel fronds, sliced stalks and chives, and drizzle with olive oil. Top with the fish and serve with the aioli and lemon wedges on the side.

Per Serve: Total carbs: 10 g | Net carbs: 6 g | Fat: 39 g | Protein: 36 g | Fat 65% | Protein 29% | Carbs 6%

Pâtés, rillettes and terrines are dishes I appreciate more and more as I get older. It feels good to eat this type of nourishing food. If you have cooked seafood ready to go, this pâté takes only a few minutes to put together. Serve with raw or pickled vegetables, seed crackers or low-carb bread or toast. It's also great on crispy seaweed or wrapped in nori.

EASY SARDINE PÂTÉ

SERVES 4

200 g jarred sardines* in brine or
    olive oil, drained
80 g (⅓ cup) Mayonnaise (page 201)
2 teaspoons lemon juice
1 tablespoon olive oil
2 tablespoons coconut oil or
    good-quality animal fat*
sea salt and freshly ground
    black pepper

To serve
4 radishes, halved
1 Lebanese cucumber, cut
    into matchsticks
4 Dutch or small carrots, cut
    into matchsticks
2 celery stalks, cut into sticks
4 okra pods, halved lengthways

* See Glossary

Place the sardines in the bowl of a food processor, then add the mayonnaise, lemon juice, olive oil and coconut oil or fat and blend to a fine paste. Season with salt and pepper. Transfer to a serving bowl, cover and place in the fridge to set for 2 hours.

Serve the pâté with the radish, cucumber, carrot, celery and okra.

Per Serve: Total carbs: 6 g | Net carbs: 4 g | Fat: 32 g | Protein: 14 g | Fat 78% | Protein 16% | Carbs 6%

Fans of Thai or Vietnamese food generally love the ubiquitous and addictive fishcakes, which have just the right balance of herbs, spices and seafood to make you come back for more. These fishcakes are baked in a muffin tray – which is so much easier than pan-frying them – then paired with lettuce cups (like san choy bao). The aromatic nam jim, so full of rich umami flavour, is the perfect accompaniment. Add chilli as desired. If you'd like to reduce the amount of carbs in these, you can replace the mashed sweet potato with mashed cauliflower.

SPICY FISHCAKES IN LETTUCE CUPS

SERVES 4

2 tablespoons coconut oil or
good-quality animal fat*, plus
extra for greasing
415 g jarred tuna, eel, mackerel,
sardines or red salmon* in
brine, drained
2 spring onions, finely chopped
1 tablespoon coriander leaves,
finely chopped
250 g mashed sweet potato
½ teaspoon finely grated lemon zest
1 long green or red chilli, halved,
deseeded and finely chopped
3 eggs
sea salt and freshly ground
black pepper

To serve
8 iceberg lettuce leaves, trimmed
into cups
1 carrot, cut into matchsticks
½ French shallot, thinly sliced
1 handful of coriander leaves
1 handful of Vietnamese mint leaves
1 handful of Thai basil leaves
1 tablespoon toasted sesame seeds
Nam Jim (page 79)

* See Glossary

Preheat the oven to 200°C (180°C fan-forced). Grease a 12-hole standard muffin tray.

Place the coconut oil or fat, jarred fish, spring onion, coriander, sweet potato, lemon zest, chilli, eggs and a pinch of salt and pepper in a bowl and mix until well combined. Spoon the mixture evenly into the holes of the prepared muffin tray. Bake for 25 minutes, or until the fishcakes are firm and cooked through. Allow them to cool in the tray for 2 minutes, before turning out onto a wire rack to cool completely.

Place the fishcakes in the iceberg lettuce cups (1–2 per cup), top with the carrot, shallot and herbs and sprinkle on the sesame seeds. Spoon over the nam jim and serve.

This is my spin on the classic Italian dish vitello tonnato – thinly sliced slow-cooked veal served with tuna mayonnaise. Here, I have replaced the veal with squid. Serve alongside some grilled broccolini or a simple salad. If squid isn't your thing, then pretty much any kind of grilled fish will work well, too.

CHARRED SQUID WITH TUNA MAYONNAISE

SERVES 2

600 g cleaned squid tubes and
    tentacles (ask your fishmonger
    to do this)
2 tablespoons melted coconut oil
    or good-quality animal fat*
sea salt and freshly ground
    black pepper

Tuna mayonnaise
100 g jarred tuna* in brine or olive oil,
    drained (or use sardines, mackerel
    or eel)
120 g Mayonnaise (page 201)
1 teaspoon lemon juice

Garlic and caper sauce
3 tablespoons coconut oil
4 garlic cloves, finely chopped
1 teaspoon finely chopped
    thyme leaves
3 tablespoons salted baby capers,
    rinsed well and patted dry
2 tablespoons lemon juice
80 ml (⅓ cup) olive oil, plus extra
    for drizzling

To serve
1 small handful of red vein sorrel or
    flat-leaf parsley leaves
1 small handful of dill fronds

* See Glossary

To make the tuna mayonnaise, place the tuna, mayonnaise and lemon juice in the bowl of a food processor and blend until smooth. Season with salt and pepper to taste. Set aside until ready to use.

Heat a large heavy-based frying pan over high heat. Coat the squid with the melted coconut oil or fat and season with salt and pepper. Place the squid in the pan and cook, tossing the pan every now and then, for 1–1½ minutes, or until cooked through and tender. Remove the squid from the pan and set aside, keeping warm.

To make the garlic and caper sauce, place the same pan over medium heat, add the coconut oil and garlic and cook for 30 seconds, or until fragrant and just starting to colour. Next, add the thyme and capers and sauté for 10 seconds. Remove from the heat, then stir in the lemon juice and olive oil. Season with salt and pepper.

To serve, spread the mayonnaise onto serving plates. Top with the squid, then spoon over the garlic and caper sauce. Scatter over the sorrel or parsley and dill, drizzle with a little extra olive oil and serve.

Per Serve: Total carbs: 7 g | Net carbs: 7 g | Fat: 58 g | Protein: 29 g | Fat 78% | Protein 18% | Carbs 4%

Steaming salmon, or any fish for that matter, is a super simple and wonderfully gentle way to evenly cook a few portions at once and enhance the flavour of the ingredients. Add some capers, pickles or kraut, if you like, or leave as is. Voila – here you have a delicious lunch or dinner with very little fuss.

STEAMED SALMON WITH FENNEL KRAUT AND ASPARAGUS

SERVES 4

4 x 150 g salmon fillets, skin off, pin-boned
sea salt and freshly ground black pepper
2 bunches of asparagus (about 440 g), woody ends trimmed
1 tablespoon extra-virgin olive oil
150 g Fennel Kraut (page 197)
4 radishes, thinly sliced
80 g Aioli (page 192)
lemon wedges, to serve

Pickled shallot
2 French shallots, thinly sliced
80 ml (⅓ cup) red wine vinegar

Place the pickled shallot ingredients in a small saucepan and bring to a simmer over medium heat. Cover with a lid and cook for 1 minute, then remove from the heat and allow to cool completely. Drain, reserving 2 tablespoons of the pickling vinegar for the dressing (save the rest for another use).

Season the salmon with salt and pepper. Fill a saucepan with 1.5 litres of water. Place a bamboo or metal steamer over the pan, line with a sheet of baking paper and bring to the boil, then reduce to a simmer. Place the salmon in the steamer, cover and steam for 4 minutes, or until the fish is still a slightly deeper pink in the centre. Remove from the steamer, cover and allow to rest, keeping warm.

Meanwhile, add the asparagus to the steamer and steam for 2 minutes, or until cooked through but still slightly crisp. Transfer to a bowl, then add the olive oil and some salt and pepper and toss to coat.

Arrange the asparagus and salmon on a serving platter or plates. Top with the fennel kraut, pickled shallot and radish and season with salt and pepper. Serve with the aioli and lemon wedges on the side.

Per Serve: Total carbs: 8 g | Net carbs: 4 g | Fat: 28 g | Protein: 33 g | Fat 62% | Protein 32% | Carbs 6%

Mackerel is fast becoming *the* darling seafood in the modern chef's repertoire. It is sustainable and, as an added bonus, is relatively inexpensive. For me, the cherry on top is that it tastes amazing. So, what do you do with mackerel when you have it? It comes up beautifully pan-fried, deep-fried, braised in curries or smoked; and works really well with strong flavours such as chilli, vinegar and citrus.

BLUE MACKEREL WITH THAI CUCUMBER SALAD

SERVES 2

4 x 70–90 g blue mackerel fillets,
    skin on, pin-boned
sea salt and freshly ground
    black pepper
2 tablespoons coconut oil or
    good-quality animal fat*
olive oil, to serve
lime wedges, to serve

Nam jim
4 red Asian shallots, chopped
2 long red chillies, chopped
2 garlic cloves, chopped
2.5 cm piece of ginger, chopped
1 tablespoon washed and finely
    chopped coriander roots and stalks
150 ml lime juice
1 tablespoon coconut sugar or honey
    (optional)
2½ tablespoons fish sauce

Thai cucumber salad
1 Lebanese cucumber, thinly sliced
1 French shallot, thinly sliced
1 long red chilli, halved lengthways,
    deseeded and cut into matchsticks
1 handful of bean sprouts
1 handful of coriander leaves
1 handful of Thai basil leaves
1 handful of mint leaves

* See Glossary

To make the nam jim, pound the shallot, chilli, garlic, ginger and coriander roots and stalks to a paste using a large mortar and pestle. Add the lime juice and mix well. Mix in the sugar or honey (if using) and fish sauce, taste and adjust the seasoning if necessary, so that the dressing is a balance of hot, sour, salty and sweet. Strain through a sieve and discard the pulp.

Season the mackerel fillets with salt and pepper. Heat a large frying pan over high heat and add the coconut oil or fat. Add the mackerel and fry, skin-side down, for 1½ minutes, then flip and cook for 15–20 seconds until the fish is just cooked through. Allow to rest for 2 minutes.

Arrange the salad ingredients on two serving plates and add the mackerel. Spoon over some nam jim, drizzle with olive oil and serve with lime wedges. Any leftover nam jim can be stored in an airtight container in the fridge for up to 1 week.

CHI

CKEN

This is a fun way to present the classic combination of chicken, bacon and avocado and to get more amazing fats into your diet, which is a key part of going keto. Obviously, eating this is going to be a bit messy. I suggest using a knife and fork rather than picking it up (well, you could try to, but maybe not on a first date). Another fun way to serve this is to put all of the ingredients into bowls on the dining table and then use nori sheets to wrap them into delicious hand rolls. This is a fantastic dish to enjoy when avocados are abundant.

CHICKEN AND BACON IN AN AVOCADO BUN

SERVES 2

2 rindless bacon rashers
2 avocados
1 baby cos lettuce, leaves
    separated and torn
300 g leftover roast
    chicken, shredded
1 teaspoon sesame seeds
freshly ground black pepper

Basil mayonnaise
3 tablespoons Mayonnaise
    (page 201)
1 teaspoon chopped basil leaves
sea salt

Preheat the oven to 200°C (180°C fan-forced). Grease and line a baking tray with baking paper.

Place the bacon in a single layer on the prepared tray, making sure the strips do not touch. Bake, turning the tray once, for 10–12 minutes until the bacon is golden brown and crisp. Keep a close eye on the bacon to prevent it from burning.

To make the avocado bun, slice each avocado in half lengthways. Remove the stone and peel away the skin. On one half of each avocado, slice off a small piece to form a flat base (this helps the bun to stand on the plate).

To make the basil mayonnaise, mix the mayonnaise and basil together and season with a pinch of salt, if needed. Set aside.

To assemble the buns, place the flat-based avocado halves on serving plates. Spread on 1 teaspoon of basil mayonnaise, then top with the bacon, cos lettuce and chicken. Spread on another teaspoon of basil mayonnaise, then add the top half of the avocado bun. Sprinkle on the sesame seeds and some pepper and serve.

Per Serve: Total carbs: 6 g | Net carbs: 2 g | Fat: 23 g | Protein: 35 g | Fat 60% | Protein 33% | Carbs 7%

I first tried this dish when I visited the Philippines on a scuba-diving holiday about 20 years ago. Obviously, being a chef, I wanted to immerse myself in the culture and learn about the local cuisine. Adobo chicken was one dish that really stood out. I learned to recreate it at home and it is now a firm family favourite. I often serve my adobo chicken with cauliflower or broccoli rice and a lovely fresh salad. Here, I've paired it with choy sum, but you could use bok choy or any other Asian greens of your choice. It's also perfect with some kimchi or spiced kraut.

ADOBO CHICKEN WINGS

SERVES 4

1 kg chicken wings
2 bunches of choy sum (about
   400 g), ends trimmed
sea salt
olive oil, for drizzling

Marinade
140 ml apple cider vinegar
100 ml tamari
6 garlic cloves, finely chopped
4 cm piece of ginger, finely grated
2 long red chillies, halved, deseeded
   and sliced
1 teaspoon freshly ground
   black pepper
1 tablespoon coconut oil
1½ tablespoons honey

To serve
1 spring onion, green part only,
   thinly sliced
2 long red chillies, sliced

To make the marinade, place all the ingredients in a large bowl with 3 tablespoons of water and mix to combine.

Add the chicken wings to the marinade and turn until the chicken is well coated. Cover and refrigerate for at least 1 hour, or ideally overnight.

Preheat the oven to 200°C (180°C fan-forced). Line a large roasting tin with baking paper.

Transfer the chicken wings and marinade to the prepared tin and spread out in a single layer. Roast, turning the wings occasionally, for 40–45 minutes until they are golden and cooked through.

Meanwhile, place the choy sum in a single layer in a steamer basket over a saucepan of boiling water. Cover and steam for about 5 minutes, or until the choy sum is tender. Season with salt and pepper and drizzle over some olive oil.

Sprinkle the spring onion and chilli over the chicken wings and serve with the steamed choy sum on the side.

I have been growing lemongrass in my garden for the last couple of years and love to use it for the beautiful aroma and flavour it imparts in my cooking. Adding lemongrass to a broth, as I have done here, creates a base for amazing Asian-inspired soups. Soups are always a great addition to your weekly menu as they are cheap, filling and nutrient dense. Feel free to add any low-carb veggies you love. The fattier cuts of chicken are best for this type of dish.

CRISPY CHICKEN IN LEMONGRASS BROTH

SERVES 4

1.5 litres Chicken Bone Broth
(page 195)
5 cm piece of ginger, sliced
4 lemongrass stems, pale part only,
    bruised and halved
4 coriander roots, washed and
    trimmed, finely chopped
4 garlic cloves, finely chopped
4 kaffir lime leaves, torn
1 tablespoon fish sauce, plus extra
    if needed
2 bunches of choy sum (about
    400 g), trimmed

Crispy chicken
4 boneless chicken thighs, skin on
sea salt
1 tablespoon coconut oil or
    good-quality animal fat*

To serve
a few coriander sprigs
1 large handful of bean sprouts
1–2 long red chillies, thinly sliced
lime cheeks

* See Glossary

Place the broth, ginger, lemongrass, coriander root, garlic, lime leaves and fish sauce in a large saucepan over medium–high heat. Bring to the boil, turn the heat to low and simmer for 30 minutes to allow the flavours to infuse. Season with more fish sauce, if needed. Add the choy sum and cook for 1½ minutes, or until tender.

Meanwhile, to make the crispy chicken, pat the chicken thighs dry with paper towel, then place between two sheets of baking paper and flatten slightly with a meat mallet. Season the skin with 2 teaspoons of salt.

Heat the coconut oil or fat in a large heavy-based frying pan over medium–high heat. Add the chicken thighs, skin-side down, and season the exposed flesh with a little salt. Fry, undisturbed, for 6–8 minutes until the skin is crispy and golden brown. Turn and cook for 3–4 minutes until cooked through. Transfer the chicken, skin-side up, to a wire rack and leave to rest for 5 minutes, before thickly slicing.

Divide the broth and choy sum among four warm serving bowls, add the chicken, coriander sprigs, bean sprouts and chilli and serve with lime cheeks on the side to squeeze over the top.

Per Serve: Total carbs: 10 g | Net carbs: 8 g | Fat: 29 g | Protein: 27 g | Fat 64% | Protein 27% | Carbs 9%

For all the fat lovers out there (me being one!), here is a fun dish that really emphasises the fat on fat philosophy by combining bacon and avocado with a piece of meat. Now, cooked avocado may seem a little strange but it adds a certain richness that is satisfying and nourishing. The bacon helps to keep the chicken moist and adds a nice crispness. Serve with a salad or side of your choice and some kraut. It's a good idea to make a few extra for work or school lunches.

CHICKEN AND GUACAMOLE WRAPPED IN BACON

SERVES 4

4 boneless chicken thighs or breasts, skin on
1 handful of rocket leaves
1 handful of baby spinach leaves
12 streaky bacon rashers
coriander leaves, to serve

Guacamole
2 avocados, diced
1 small red chilli, halved, deseeded and finely chopped, plus extra to serve (optional)
juice of 1 lime, or more to taste
1 tablespoon finely diced red onion
2 tablespoons chopped coriander leaves
1 tablespoon extra-virgin olive oil
sea salt and freshly ground black pepper

Preheat the oven to 220°C (200°C fan-forced).

To make the guacamole, combine all the ingredients in a small bowl and mash with a fork.

Lightly season the chicken with salt and pepper. Place the chicken between two sheets of baking paper and pound with a meat mallet until about 1 cm thick.

Spoon 3 tablespoons of guacamole in the centre of each flattened chicken piece, add some rocket and spinach and season with a little salt and pepper. Roll the chicken around the filling. Wrap each chicken piece tightly in three strips of bacon and thread a couple of toothpicks through the bacon seams to secure.

Place the chicken on a baking tray and roast for 25 minutes, or until the bacon is golden brown and the chicken is cooked through. Set aside to rest for 5 minutes.

Cut the chicken into 2 cm thick slices, scatter over the coriander leaves and extra chilli (if using) and serve.

Per Serve: Total carbs: 8 g | Net carbs: 3 g | Fat: 46 g | Protein: 23 g | Fat 79% | Protein 16% | Carbs 5%

Chicken and ginger in a stir-fry are a match made in culinary heaven. And everyone in your family will love this combination. Serve with any vegetables you like and spice it up with some chilli if you feel like a kick. I serve it with cauliflower rice as a great keto addition.

GINGER CHICKEN STIR-FRY

SERVES 4

3 tablespoons coconut oil or
  good-quality animal fat*
700 g boneless chicken thighs,
  skin on, cut into 3 cm pieces
4 spring onions, cut into 5 cm batons
300 g broccoli, broken into florets
1 carrot, cut into matchsticks
2 baby bok choy, roughly chopped
5 shiitake mushrooms, sliced
sea salt and freshly ground
  black pepper

Stir-fry sauce

1 tablespoon coconut oil or
  good-quality animal fat
4 garlic cloves, finely chopped
6 cm piece of ginger, cut into
  matchsticks
1 long red chilli, halved, deseeded and
  cut into matchsticks
250 ml (1 cup) Chicken Bone Broth
  (page 195)
3 tablespoons tamari
1 tablespoon coconut sugar or honey
2 teaspoons toasted sesame oil
2 teaspoons sesame seeds
½ teaspoon freshly ground
  black pepper
2 teaspoons tapioca flour* whisked
  with 1 tablespoon water

To serve

Cauliflower Rice (page 194)
toasted sesame seeds
coriander leaves
lime cheeks

* See Glossary

To make the stir-fry sauce, heat the coconut oil or fat in a saucepan over medium heat. Add the garlic, ginger and chilli and cook until fragrant, about 1 minute. Pour in the broth and tamari, add the coconut sugar or honey, sesame oil, sesame seeds and pepper and bring to a simmer. Whisk in the tapioca mixture, bring to the boil and simmer for 1 minute. Remove from the heat and set aside until needed.

Melt 1 tablespoon of the coconut oil or fat in a wok or large heavy-based frying pan over high heat. Working in batches, sauté the chicken for 4½–5 minutes until just browned and cooked through. Transfer to a plate.

Add the remaining coconut oil or fat to the pan along with the spring onion and stir-fry for 1½ minutes, or until just turning brown. Add the rest of the vegetables and stir-fry for 5 minutes or so until they reach your preferred level of crunch. Return the chicken to the pan. Pour in the stir-fry sauce, mix everything together and cook for 1–2 minutes. Season with salt and pepper, if needed.

Divide the cauliflower rice among four serving bowls and top with the stir-fry. Sprinkle over some sesame seeds and coriander leaves and serve with lime cheeks on the side.

Your meals needn't be difficult or expensive but they should always be delicious. Here, we have one of the simplest recipes in the book, and it is sure to be a winner. Make a big batch of these (you can do this in a muffin tray if you like), as they are wonderful to have on hand for snacks and lunches.

CHICKEN BURGERS WITH GARLIC, LEMON AND THYME

SERVES 4

2 baby cos lettuces, leaves separated
100 g Mayonnaise (page 201)
1 lemon, cut into wedges

Chicken burgers
3 tablespoons coconut oil or
   good-quality animal fat*
½ onion, finely diced
3 garlic cloves, finely chopped
1 teaspoon chopped thyme leaves
500 g chicken mince
1 egg
1 tablespoon chopped flat-leaf
   parsley leaves
zest of 1 lemon
1 teaspoon sea salt
½ teaspoon freshly ground
   black pepper

* See Glossary

To make the burgers, heat 1 tablespoon of the coconut oil or fat in a frying pan over medium heat. Add the onion and cook for 5 minutes, or until softened. Add the garlic and thyme and cook for 30 seconds, or until fragrant. Remove from the heat and allow to cool.

Place the cooled onion mixture in a bowl, then add the remaining burger ingredients and mix well. Shape into eight patties.

Heat the remaining coconut oil or fat in a large non-stick frying pan over medium–high heat. Add the patties, in batches if necessary, and cook for 2½–3 minutes on each side until they are cooked through.

Place the patties on the cos leaves and top with the mayonnaise. Serve with lemon wedges to squeeze over the top.

     Per Serve: Total carbs: 4 g | Net carbs: 3 g | Fat: 41 g | Protein: 27 g | Fat 75% | Protein 22% | Carbs 3%

A lot of my books feature chicken salads because they are just so damned delicious. Also, they are an easy, quick and tasty way to use up leftover roast chicken. Take whatever leafy greens you love the most and make that your base, then add the chicken, vegetables or fruit and some crunchy seeds or nuts, fresh herbs and kraut. Dress, add some good fats, such as avocado, olives or hard-boiled eggs, and you're done.

CRISPY CHICKEN SALAD WITH TOASTED WALNUTS

SERVES 4

4 boneless chicken thighs,
   skin on
sea salt and freshly ground black
   pepper
1 tablespoon coconut oil or
   good-quality animal fat*
extra-virgin olive oil, for drizzling

Dressing
100 g Mayonnaise (page 201)
1½ tablespoons lemon juice
¼ teaspoon grated garlic

Salad
400 g savoy cabbage, shredded
2 large handfuls of baby
   spinach leaves
½ red onion, finely chopped
1 pink lady apple, cored and cut
   into matchsticks
1 handful of mint leaves, torn
1 handful of flat-leaf parsley leaves
1 handful of chervil leaves
1 handful of tarragon leaves
100 g toasted walnuts

* See Glossary

To make the crispy chicken, pat the chicken thighs dry with paper towel, then place between two sheets of baking paper and flatten with a meat mallet. Season the skin with 2 teaspoons of salt.

Heat the coconut oil or fat in a large heavy-based frying pan over medium–high heat. Add the chicken thighs, skin-side down, and season the exposed flesh with a little salt. Fry, undisturbed, for 6–8 minutes until the skin is crispy and golden brown. Turn and cook for 3–4 minutes until cooked through. Transfer the chicken, skin-side up, to a wire rack and leave to rest for 5 minutes. Chop into bite-sized pieces.

To make the dressing, place the mayonnaise, lemon juice, garlic and 2 teaspoons of water in a small bowl and mix to combine. Season with salt and pepper.

Arrange all the salad ingredients in a large bowl, top with the chicken, then pour over the dressing. Drizzle over some olive oil and season with salt and pepper. Give the salad a good toss before eating.

Per Serve: Total carbs: 16 g | Net carbs: 9 g | Fat: 66 g | Protein: 26 g | Fat 78% | Protein 14% | Carbs 8%

Zhoug, a delicious hot sauce with origins in Yemeni-Jewish cuisine, is popular all around the world. And rightly so, as the addictive flavours and harmony of spices dance on the tongue. Similar to chimichurri sauce, zhoug is the perfect accompaniment to grilled meats and seafood, and egg and vegetable dishes. If you want to mellow it a little, simply fold through some mayo.

CHICKEN WINGS WITH ZHOUG

SERVES 4

1 kg chicken wings
1 red onion, cut into wedges

Marinade
2 tablespoons melted coconut oil
   or good-quality animal fat*
2 garlic cloves, finely chopped
1 teaspoon ground turmeric
1 tablespoon apple cider vinegar
sea salt and freshly ground
   black pepper

Zhoug
45 g (1½ cups) coriander leaves
2 large handfuls of flat-leaf
   parsley leaves
2 jalapeño chillies, halved, deseeded
   and chopped (keep the seeds in
   if you like it spicy)
1 garlic clove, chopped
3 tablespoons olive oil
½ teaspoon ground cumin
½ teaspoon ground coriander
3 teaspoons apple cider vinegar

To serve
oregano leaves
lemon wedges

* See Glossary

To make the marinade, combine the coconut oil or fat, garlic, turmeric, vinegar, a pinch of salt and pepper and 2 tablespoons of water in a large bowl and whisk well.

Add the chicken wings to the marinade and turn until the chicken is well coated. Cover and refrigerate for at least 1 hour or, ideally, overnight.

Preheat the oven to 220°C (200°C fan-forced).

Transfer the wings and the marinade to a roasting tin and spread out in a single layer. Add the red onion and roast, turning the wings and onion occasionally, for 40–45 minutes until the chicken is golden brown and cooked through.

Meanwhile, to make the zhoug, place the herbs, chilli and garlic in the bowl of a food processor and blend until finely chopped. With the motor running, pour in the oil, whiz until combined, then pour in 3 tablespoons of water and process until incorporated. Add the spices and vinegar and season with salt and pepper to taste. Process until well blended. Set aside until needed.

Arrange the chicken wings and onion on a serving platter, pour over the juices in the roasting tin, then scatter over some oregano leaves and dollop on some zhoug. Serve with lemon wedges and the remaining zhoug on the side.

Souvlaki is a traditional Greek dish of seasoned grilled meat that is cooked until tender and juicy. I am a huge fan of using chicken thighs with the skin on, as they have more flavour than breast meat and stay lovely and succulent. Alternatively, you can use liver, heart or any other protein.

CHICKEN SOUVLAKI WITH GREEK SALAD

SERVES 4

sea salt and freshly ground
    black pepper
8 boneless chicken thighs, skin on,
    cut into 2.5 cm cubes
lemon wedges, to serve

Tzatziki
½ Lebanese cucumber, grated
200 g Coconut Yoghurt (page 196)
1 tablespoon extra-virgin olive oil
1 tablespoon finely chopped mint
    leaves
1 teaspoon finely chopped dill fronds
1 garlic clove, finely grated
1 teaspoon lemon juice, or to taste

Marinade
3 tablespoons melted coconut oil or
    good-quality animal fat*
zest and juice of 1 lemon
1 tablespoon finely grated garlic
1 tablespoon red wine vinegar
1 teaspoon honey (optional)
2½ teaspoons dried oregano
1 teaspoon dried thyme
1 teaspoon ground cumin
½ teaspoon sweet paprika

Greek salad
1 Lebanese cucumber, halved
    lengthways and sliced
2 roma tomatoes, cut into wedges
¼ red onion, thinly sliced
1 baby cos lettuce, quartered and
    leaves separated
2 tablespoons red wine vinegar
3 tablespoons extra-virgin olive oil

* See Glossary

Combine all the tzatziki ingredients in a bowl, season with salt and mix well. Cover and place in the fridge until ready to use.

Combine all the marinade ingredients in a large bowl, season with salt and pepper whisk well.

Add the chicken to the marinade and toss until thoroughly coated. Cover and place in the fridge to marinate for 1–2 hours.

Meanwhile, soak eight bamboo skewers in cold water for 20 minutes. Drain.

Thread the marinated chicken onto the prepared skewers, about 4 pieces per skewer, and season with salt and pepper.

Heat a barbecue grill plate to medium–hot or a large chargrill pan over medium–high heat. Brush with a little coconut oil or fat and cook the chicken, turning occasionally, for 10–12 minutes or until cooked through.

To make the salad, place the cucumber, tomato, onion and lettuce in a bowl. In a small bowl, whisk together the vinegar and olive oil, then pour over the salad and toss. Season with salt and pepper.

To serve, arrange the chicken souvlaki skewers on a platter and serve with the tzatziki, Greek salad and lemon wedges.

Per Serve: Total carbs: 15 g | Net carbs: 11 g | Fat: 66 g | Protein: 34 g | Fat 76% | Protein 17% | Carbs 7%

Sichuan peppercorns are one of the most unique and tantalising spices on the planet, and they go particularly well with chicken. Sichuan peppercorns can tingle on the tongue and sometimes even make the mouth go numb – an unusual but fun experience.

SICHUAN CRACKLING CHICKEN

SERVES 4

4 boneless chicken thighs, skin on
sea salt
2 tablespoons coconut oil or
    good-quality animal fat*
1 zucchini, spiralised
2 Lebanese cucumbers, spiralised
2 carrots, spiralised
½ daikon, spiralised
1 handful of bean sprouts
4 spring onions, sliced
½ teaspoon chilli flakes (add more
    if you like it extra spicy)
1 handful of coriander leaves

Sichuan dressing

2 tablespoons coconut sugar
3 tablespoons tamari
3 tablespoons apple cider vinegar
1 tablespoon unhulled tahini
1 teaspoon sesame oil
1 tablespoon chilli oil
1 tablespoon olive oil
80 ml (⅓ cup) Chicken Bone Broth
    (page 195)
1 teaspoon finely grated ginger
1 teaspoon Sichuan peppercorns,
    toasted and ground

* See Glossary

Pat the chicken thighs dry with paper towel, then place between two sheets of baking paper and pound with a meat mallet until about 1 cm thick. Season the skin with 2 teaspoons of salt.

Heat the coconut oil or fat in a large heavy-based frying pan over medium heat. Add the chicken, skin-side down and in batches, season the exposed flesh with a little salt and fry, undisturbed, for 6–8 minutes until crispy and golden brown. Flip the chicken over and cook for 3–4 minutes until the chicken is cooked through. Transfer the chicken, skin-side up, to a wire rack and leave to rest for 5 minutes, before thickly slicing.

To make the dressing, combine the coconut sugar (if using), tamari and vinegar in a bowl, mix well and stand for a few minutes to allow the sugar to dissolve. Whisk in the tahini, then whisk in the oils and broth. Add the ginger and ground peppercorns and set aside.

Arrange the zucchini, cucumber, carrot, daikon and bean sprouts on serving plates. Place the chicken on top, then pour over the dressing and sprinkle on the spring onion, chilli flakes and coriander leaves.

NOTE
If you don't have a spiraliser, finely slice the zucchini, cucumber, carrots and daikon lengthways, then cut into thin strips.

Per Serve: Total carbs: 14 g | Net carbs: 9 g | Fat: 37 g | Protein: 25 g | Fat 70% | Protein 19% | Carbs 11%

This simple recipe showcases lemon and chicken. A treat to prepare and eat, the juices from the lemon and chicken mix to create the most delicious sauce. I advise cooking extra as the chicken is perfect for salads, snacks and sandwich fillings. Of course, you can use chicken thighs with the skin on instead.

ROASTED CHICKEN BREAST WITH LEMON, THYME AND GARLIC

SERVES 4

4 chicken breasts with wing bone,
   skin on
sea salt and freshly ground
   black pepper
2 tablespoons coconut oil or
   good-quality animal fat*
4 garlic cloves, finely chopped
2 teaspoons finely chopped
   thyme leaves
2 teaspoons dried oregano
zest and juice of 1 lemon
2 tablespoons olive oil, plus extra
   to serve
1½ baby cos lettuces, leaves separated
lemon wedges, to serve

* See Glossary

Preheat the oven to 200°C (180°C fan-forced).

Season the chicken generously with salt and pepper.

Heat the coconut oil or fat in a large ovenproof frying pan over medium–high heat. Seal the chicken, skin-side down, for 3 minutes, or until the skin is golden and crisp. Flip over and seal the other side for 1 minute, or until golden. Flip the chicken again and transfer the pan to the oven for 5 minutes.

Meanwhile, place the garlic, thyme, oregano, lemon zest and juice and olive oil in a small bowl and mix well.

Remove the pan from the oven and pour the garlic and lemon dressing over the chicken. Continue to roast the chicken for a further 5–6 minutes until cooked through. Set aside to rest for 5 minutes, then thickly slice.

Divide the cos leaves among four serving plates. Add the chicken and spoon over the juices in the pan. Drizzle some olive oil over the lettuce and squeeze on some lemon juice from the wedges.

ME

AT

Meat muffins are perfect any time of day and make a wonderful keto addition to school and work lunch boxes. Super easy to make in bulk, they are inexpensive and very tasty. You can pretty much flavour them with whatever spices or seasonings you love, taking inspiration from all over the globe. These beef muffins are seductively spiced with Indian flavours. I love to eat them with some kraut or pickles on the side.

CURRIED BEEF AND VEGGIE MUFFINS

SERVES 4

2 tablespoons coconut oil or
    good-quality animal fat*,
    plus extra for greasing
3 garlic cloves, finely chopped
1 onion, finely chopped
500 g beef mince
1 egg
60 g (½ cup) grated sweet potato
80 g (½ cup) grated carrot
2 tablespoons chopped flat-leaf
    parsley leaves
2½ tablespoons curry powder
1 tablespoon tomato paste
1 tablespoon tamari
80 ml (⅓ cup) Chicken Bone Broth
    (page 195)
sea salt and freshly ground
    black pepper
lemon wedges, to serve

Cucumber salad
½ teaspoon each of cumin seeds,
    yellow mustard seeds and
    coriander seeds
1 teaspoon coconut oil
2 tablespoons lemon juice
3 tablespoons extra-virgin olive oil
2 Lebanese cucumbers, thinly sliced
1 handful of mint leaves, chopped

Curried aioli
150 g Aioli (page 192)
1 teaspoon curry powder

* See Glossary

Preheat the oven to 200°C (180°C fan-forced). Lightly grease a 12-hole standard muffin tray with coconut oil or fat.

Heat the coconut oil or fat in a frying pan over medium heat. Add the garlic and onion and sauté, stirring occasionally, for 6 minutes, or until browned. Remove from the heat and set aside.

Combine the mince, egg, sweet potato, carrot, parsley, curry powder, tomato paste, tamari and broth in a bowl. Add the onion mixture, season with a pinch of salt and pepper and combine well. Spoon the mixture evenly into the holes of the prepared muffin tray. Bake for 15 minutes, or until the meaty muffins are perfectly juicy.

To make the cucumber salad, using a mortar and pestle, lightly crush the cumin, mustard and coriander seeds. Heat the coconut oil in a small frying pan over medium heat, add the spices and cook for 20–30 seconds until fragrant and toasted. Place in a bowl, then add the lemon juice and olive oil and whisk to combine. Season with salt and pepper. Add the cucumber and mint, toss and spoon into a serving bowl.

To make the curried aioli, place the aioli and curry powder in a bowl and mix to combine.

Serve the muffins with the cucumber salad and curried aioli on the side, and with lemon wedges for squeezing over.

Per Serve: Total carbs: 14 g | Net carbs: 12 g | Fat: 44 g | Protein: 30 g | Fat 70% | Protein 21% | Carbs 9%

I am a firm believer that we should include kangaroo in our diet as there is a huge supply of them and their meat is simple to prepare. Some native cultures believe we take on the energy of the animals we consume, so would hunt the most athletic and powerful creatures. Have a think about your diet; is what you consume caged or free range, wild or farmed? To me, this is food for thought, and one reason why I like to include protein from wild land and sea animals in my diet.

SPICED KANGAROO FILLET WITH FATTOUSH

SERVES 6

2 Keto Flatbreads (page 200)
3 tablespoons extra-virgin olive oil, plus extra to serve
sea salt and freshly ground black pepper
2½ teaspoons za'atar*
4 x 160 g kangaroo fillets
1 tablespoons baharat* or ground cumin
3 tablespoons coconut oil or good-quality animal fat*
1 tablespoon chopped toasted pumpkin seeds
Cauliflower Hummus (page 194)
1½ baby cos lettuces, leaves separated

Fattoush

3 large tomatoes (about 400 g), deseeded and cut into 1.5 cm dice
1½ Lebanese cucumbers, deseeded and cut into 1.5 cm dice
4 radishes, cut into 1.5 cm dice
½ red capsicum, cut into 1.5 cm dice
½ red onion, finely chopped
1 handful each of flat-leaf parsley and mint leaves, roughly chopped
80 g pomegranate seeds

Dressing

1 garlic clove, finely grated
3 tablespoons lemon juice
80 ml (⅓ cup) extra-virgin olive oil
1 teaspoon sumac*, plus extra to serve

* See Glossary

Preheat the oven to 200°C (180°C fan-forced). Line two large baking trays with baking paper.

Place the flatbreads on the prepared trays in a single layer. Brush each one with about 1 teaspoon of olive oil, sprinkle on some salt and about ¼ teaspoon of za'atar. Toast in the oven for 8–10 minutes until lightly golden and crisp. Keep an eye on them after 6 minutes, as they can burn quickly.

Rub the baharat or cumin over the kangaroo fillets, season with salt and pepper and set aside.

Heat the coconut oil or fat in a large frying pan over medium–high heat. Working in two batches, add the fillets and cook, turning, for 5 minutes, or until cooked to your liking. Rest, lightly covered with a cloth, for 5 minutes.

Toss together the fattoush ingredients in a large bowl.

Combine the dressing ingredients in a small bowl and mix well.

Pour the dressing over the fattoush, toss well and season with salt and pepper.

Slice the kangaroo, arrange on a platter and sprinkle over some za'atar and the pumpkin seeds. Spoon the cauliflower hummus into a serving bowl, then drizzle on some olive oil and sprinkle over the remaining za'atar and some sumac. Arrange the fattoush in another serving bowl, rip the bread into pieces and pile on one side of the salad. Serve with the cos leaves on the side.

The beautiful thing about a nutrient-dense egg bake like this is that you can make it in advance for the days ahead. Experiment with flavours for different taste sensations. The choices really are endless and come down to your imagination. Serve with a salad of your choice and some kraut.

SAUSAGE AND CABBAGE BAKE

SERVES 6

2 tablespoons coconut oil or
   good-quality animal fat*
5 paleo sausages of your choice
250 g rindless bacon rashers,
   chopped
1 onion, chopped
4 garlic cloves, finely chopped
600 g savoy cabbage, sliced
150 g Brussels sprouts, sliced
250 ml (1 cup) Chicken Bone Broth
   (page 195)
sea salt and freshly ground
   black pepper
8 eggs
250 ml (1 cup) coconut cream
1 tablespoons Dijon mustard

* See Glossary

Preheat the oven to 180°C (160°C fan-forced).

Heat 1 tablespoon of the coconut oil or fat in a large frying pan over medium–high heat. Add the sausages and seal on all sides until browned but still raw in the middle, about 3 minutes. Remove from the heat. When cool enough to handle, cut the sausages into bite-sized pieces. Set aside until needed.

Add the bacon to the same pan and fry over medium–high heat until golden, about 5 minutes. Remove from the pan and set aside until needed.

Wipe the pan clean, add the remaining coconut oil or fat and place over medium heat. Add the onion and sauté for 5 minutes, or until softened. Add the garlic and cook for 1 minute, or until fragrant. Stir in the cabbage, Brussels sprouts and 125 ml of broth and sauté for 5 minutes to soften. Season with salt and pepper.

Place the cabbage mixture in a bowl, then add the bacon and sausage and give it a good mix.

Crack the eggs into another bowl, then add the coconut cream, remaining broth and the mustard and whisk well until smooth. Season with salt and pepper.

Tip the sautéed veg and sausage mixture into a casserole dish and spread out to form an even layer, then pour over the egg mixture. Bake for 15 minutes, then rotate the dish and bake for a further 15 minutes, or until the egg is golden on top and set in the middle. Allow to rest for 5 minutes before serving.

Per Serve: Total carbs: 15 g | Net carbs: 10 g | Fat: 41 g | Protein: 33 g | Fat 66% | Protein 24% | Carbs 10%

Cranking up the barbecue and cooking chops is one of the fondest memories I have of growing up in Australia in the '70s and '80s. Everyone ate them and felt comfortable cooking them, and they always tasted good. Serving the humble chop with the classic French dish ratatouille is a stroke of culinary genius. If you feel like a change, you could easily try an Italian caponata instead, or a cooked German sauerkraut, or some grilled broccolini or a simple salad. Perfect!

PORK CHOPS WITH RATATOUILLE

SERVES 4

4 x 200 g pork cutlets
2 tablespoons melted coconut oil
    or good-quality animal fat*
1 handful of basil leaves

Ratatouille

300 ml coconut oil or good-quality
    animal fat*
1 large eggplant, cut into 2 cm pieces
2 zucchini, cut into 2 cm pieces
1 red onion, diced
1 red capsicum, cut into 2 cm pieces
5 tomatoes, chopped
2 garlic cloves, chopped
2 tablespoons apple cider vinegar
3 tablespoons olive oil
sea salt and freshly ground
    black pepper

* See Glossary

To make the ratatouille, heat the coconut oil or fat in a large heavy-based frying pan over medium–high heat until it starts to smoke. Add the eggplant and fry until golden, about 4–5 minutes. Remove the eggplant with a slotted spoon and drain on paper towel. Repeat with the zucchini. Reserve the leftover oil. Heat 2 tablespoons of the reserved oil in a large saucepan over medium heat. Add the onion and cook, stirring occasionally, for 5 minutes, or until softened. Stir in the capsicum, tomato, garlic and 3 tablespoons of water and cook, stirring now and then, for 8 minutes, or until softened. Stir in the fried eggplant and zucchini and gently simmer for 15 minutes, or until the tomato has broken down into a rich sauce. Stir in the vinegar and olive oil and season with salt and pepper.

Coat the pork cutlets with the coconut oil or fat and season with salt and pepper

Heat a large heavy-based frying pan over medium–high heat, add the pork and cook, turning occasionally, for 6–8 minutes, or until browned and just cooked through. Allow to rest for 5 minutes.

To serve, divide the ratatouille among serving plates, place a pork cutlet on top and scatter over the basil.

Per Serve: Total carbs: 23 g | Net carbs: 15 g | Fat: 108 g | Protein: 62 g | Fat 74% | Protein 20% | Carbs 6%

I absolutely adore the combination of sausages, onion, bacon and gravy. And I encourage you to try this at home. I love juicy pork sausages for this dish, as they have a fatty quality that is perfect for a ketogenic approach. If you want to lower the carbs, then simply serve with cauliflower mash (page 194) and green veggies, such as broccolini, kale, spinach or silverbeet.

PORK SAUSAGES WITH ONION AND BACON GRAVY

SERVES 4

4 rindless streaky bacon rashers
1.5 litres Beef Bone Broth
   (page 193)
2 tablespoons coconut oil or
   good-quality animal fat*
8 paleo pork sausages
1½ onions, sliced
1 tablespoon tomato paste
5 thyme sprigs, leaves picked
100 ml red wine (such as shiraz)
1 tablespoon Worcestershire sauce
sea salt and freshly ground black
   pepper
Parsnip and Cauliflower Mash
   (page 202)
chopped flat-leaf parsley leaves,
   to serve

* See Glossary

Preheat the oven to 200°C (180°C fan-forced).

Place the bacon on a baking tray and bake for 10 minutes. Flip the bacon and cook for a further 8–10 minutes until golden brown and crisp. When cool enough to handle, chop the bacon into small pieces.

Pour the broth into a saucepan, bring to the boil and cook for 20–25 minutes until reduced to 400 ml. Remove from the heat and set aside.

Heat the coconut oil or fat in a large, deep frying pan over medium heat. Add the sausages and cook for about 8 minutes, or until browned on all sides and almost cooked through. Remove the sausages from the pan and set aside.

Using the same pan and the fat left over from cooking the sausages, sauté the onion over medium heat for 10–12 minutes until caramelised. Add the tomato paste, then add the thyme and red wine and cook, stirring constantly, for 3 minutes, or until the liquid has evaporated. Gradually pour in the reduced broth and Worcestershire sauce, stirring constantly. Bring to the boil and simmer for 5–6 minutes, or until the sauce is thickened. Stir in the bacon and season with salt and pepper. Return the sausages to the pan and cook for 2 minutes, or until they are completely cooked through.

Divide the mash among four serving dishes. Top with the sausages, then spoon over the onion and bacon gravy. Sprinkle on the parsley and finish with a good grind of pepper.

Meatballs cooked in tomato sauce is a mid-week winner that will have the whole family rejoicing. Any leftovers make for a delicious breakfast or lunch the next day. If you want to shake things up, serve with paleo buns (page 201) for your own take on a sub sandwich.

ITALIAN-STYLE MEATBALLS WITH MASH

SERVES 4

3 tablespoons coconut oil or
    good-quality animal fat*
½ onion, finely chopped
3 garlic cloves, finely chopped
1 teaspoon fennel seeds, crushed
450 g pork mince
200 g beef mince
3 tablespoons chopped flat-leaf
    parsley leaves
1 egg
2 tablespoons almond meal
¼ teaspoon chilli flakes (optional)
Cauliflower Mash (page 194), to serve

Tomato and basil sauce
1 tablespoon coconut oil or
    good-quality animal fat*
1 onion, chopped
4 garlic cloves, crushed
2 tablespoons tomato paste
400 g whole peeled tomatoes,
    crushed (see Note page 163)
400 ml Chicken Bone Broth
    (page 195) or water
1 teaspoon dried oregano
6 basil leaves, torn, plus extra to serve
sea salt and freshly ground
    black pepper
2 tablespoons extra-virgin olive oil

* See Glossary

To make the tomato and basil sauce, heat the coconut oil or fat in a saucepan over medium heat. Add the onion and cook for 5 minutes, or until softened. Add the garlic and tomato paste and sauté for 1 minute, or until fragrant. Add the tomatoes, broth or water, oregano and basil and bring to a simmer. Reduce the heat to medium–low and cook for 30 minutes, or until the sauce is rich in flavour. Season with salt and pepper, then blend until smooth with a hand-held blender and mix in the olive oil.

Meanwhile, to make the meatballs, heat half the coconut oil or fat in a large frying pan over medium heat. Add the onion and cook for 5 minutes, or until translucent. Add the garlic and fennel seeds and cook for 1 minute, or until the garlic starts to colour. Remove from the heat and allow to cool.

In a large bowl, mix the pork and beef mince with the cooked onion mixture, the parsley, egg, almond meal, chilli flakes (if using) and some salt and pepper until well incorporated. Place the bowl in the fridge for 30 minutes, so that the meatball mixture will be easier to roll.

Roll the meatball mixture into walnut-sized portions. Heat the remaining coconut oil or fat in a large frying pan over medium–high heat. Add the meatballs, in batches if necessary, and fry for about 3 minutes, or until golden. Pour in the tomato and basil sauce and bring to a simmer. Reduce the heat to medium–low, cover and simmer for 15–18 minutes until the meatballs are cooked through.

Spoon the mash onto serving plates, add the meatballs and sauce and serve with the extra basil leaves and a grind of black pepper.

Per Serve: Total carbs: 14 g | Net carbs: 11 g | Fat: 46 g | Protein: 38 g | Fat 67% | Protein 24% | Carbs 9%

From the time humans learned to control fire, cooking huge chunks of meat has been an integral part of our evolution. Large pieces of meat are often cheaper, easier to cook and more delicious than leaner cuts. They favour long and slow cooking, which is a wonderful way to impart flavour.

JAMAICAN PULLED PORK

SERVES 8

1 x 2 kg boned pork shoulder, trimmed
3 tablespoons coconut oil or good-quality animal fat*
sea salt and freshly ground black pepper
5 garlic cloves, peeled
2 onions, chopped
2 teaspoons finely grated ginger
2 tablespoons tamari
280 ml Barbecue Sauce (page 192)
500 ml (2 cups) Chicken Bone Broth (page 195) or water
dried chilli flakes, to serve (optional)
lime wedges, to serve

Jerk spice mix
1 tablespoon garlic powder
½ teaspoon cayenne pepper
2 teaspoons onion powder
2 teaspoons dried thyme
2 teaspoons dried parsley
3 teaspoons smoked paprika
1 teaspoon ground allspice
½ teaspoon ground nutmeg
¼ teaspoon ground cinnamon

Simple cabbage slaw
½ red cabbage, shredded
3 tablespoons extra-virgin olive oil
juice of 1 lime

* See Glossary

To make the jerk spice mix, place all the ingredients in a bowl along with 2 teaspoons of salt and ½ teaspoon of freshly ground black pepper. Mix well.

Rinse the pork and pat dry with paper towel. Cut the pork in half, then rub with 1 tablespoon of the coconut oil or fat. Rub the jerk spice mix over the pork and sprinkle with salt and pepper. Place on a tray, cover and refrigerate overnight.

Place the garlic, onion and ginger in a food processor and whiz for 30 seconds to form a paste.

Heat 1 tablespoon of the remaining coconut oil or fat in a large frying pan over high heat, add the pork and seal for 4 minutes on all sides. Remove from the heat.

Preheat the oven to 140°C (120°C fan-forced).

Heat the remaining oil or fat in a large flameproof casserole dish over medium heat. Add the onion paste and cook, stirring occasionally, for 5 minutes, or until fragrant. Remove from the heat, add the pork and pour in the tamari, barbecue sauce and broth or water. Cover and bake for 4½–5 hours until the meat is falling apart. Remove the meat from the dish and shred with two forks.

Preheat the oven grill to high. Place the shredded pork in a deep baking tray in a single layer and grill for 3–4 minutes until crispy and golden.

Place the casserole dish over medium–high heat and simmer until the pork juices reduce to a thick sauce consistency. Set aside, keeping warm.

Combine all the cabbage slaw ingredients in a large bowl and season with salt and pepper.

Mix the sauce through the pork, sprinkle over some dried chilli (if using) and serve with the slaw and lime wedges. Leftover pulled pork can be stored in the freezer for up to 3 months.

Per Serve: Total carbs: 13 g | Net carbs: 11 g | Fat: 57 g | Protein: 60 g | Fat 63% | Protein 31% | Carbs 6%

I often cook with lamb mince, as it is so tasty and the cuisines that it lends itself to are plentiful: think Middle Eastern, Greek, Italian and French. You really can't go wrong – and kids love it too. If I am increasing my carbs to break out of ketosis, I sometimes add sweet potato fries to these.

LAMB, MINT AND ROSEMARY PATTIES

SERVES 4

2 tablespoons coconut oil or
   good-quality animal fat*,
   plus extra for greasing
1 onion, finely chopped
3 garlic cloves, finely chopped
1 teaspoon ground cumin
½ teaspoon chilli flakes (optional)
170 g cherry tomatoes on the vine,
   snipped into 4 bunches
1 tablespoon olive oil
600 g lamb mince
150 g lamb or pork fat, minced
   (ask your butcher)
1 tablespoon dried mint
1 tablespoon finely chopped
   rosemary leaves
2 eggs, lightly beaten

Yoghurt sauce
100 g Coconut Yoghurt (page 196)
3 tablespoons Mayonnaise (page 201)
¼ teaspoon finely grated garlic
pinch of ground cumin
2 teaspoons lemon juice, or to taste
2 teaspoons finely chopped dill fronds
sea salt and freshly ground
   black pepper

Cucumber salad
1 Lebanese cucumber, halved
   lengthways and sliced
1 handful of mint leaves
1 large handful of rocket leaves
¼ red onion, thinly sliced
1½ tablespoons lemon juice
3 tablespoons olive oil

* See Glossary

Preheat the oven to 200°C (180°C fan-forced). Line a baking tray with baking paper.

Place all the yoghurt sauce ingredients in a bowl, mix to combine and season with salt and pepper to taste.

Heat 1 tablespoon of the coconut oil or fat in a frying pan over medium heat. Add the onion and sauté for 5 minutes, or until softened. Add the garlic and cook for a further minute, then stir in the cumin and chilli flakes (if using) and cook for 30 seconds, or until fragrant. Set aside to cool.

Place the cherry tomato bunches on the prepared tray, drizzle over the olive oil and sprinkle on some salt and pepper. Bake for 12 minutes, or until the tomatoes are softened and the skins start to blister.

Meanwhile, in a large bowl, mix the lamb mince, lamb or pork fat, herbs, eggs, a little salt and pepper and the cooked onion mixture until well incorporated. Shape into eight patties.

Heat the remaining coconut oil or fat in a large non-stick frying pan over medium heat. Add the patties and cook for 3 minutes until browned. Turn the patties and continue to cook for 3 minutes, or until they are cooked through.

To make the salad, place the cucumber, mint, rocket and onion in a bowl. Add the lemon juice and olive oil and gently toss. Season with salt and pepper.

Serve the patties with the roasted tomato bunches, cucumber salad and yoghurt sauce on the side.

Per Serve: Total carbs: 14 g | Net carbs: 11 g | Fat: 76 g | Protein: 45 g | Fat 75% | Protein 20% | Carbs 5%

This really simple recipe adds a lot of flavour to the humble pork fillet. You could easily do the same thing with a pork cutlet or, even better, pork neck, belly or shank (just be aware that these cuts require more cooking time).

LEMONGRASS PORK WITH NAM JIM JAEW

SERVES 4

600 g pork fillets
melted coconut oil or good-quality
    animal fat*, for drizzling
lime cheeks, to serve

Marinade

2 lemongrass stems, pale part only,
    coarsely chopped
4 coriander roots, washed and
    trimmed
4 garlic cloves, peeled
freshly ground black pepper
2 teaspoons coconut sugar (optional)
2 tablespoons fish sauce
2 tablespoons tamari

Nam jim jaew

1 tablespoon tamarind pulp*
8 long red chillies, halved, deseeded
    and chopped
2 garlic cloves, chopped
80 ml (⅓ cup) fish sauce
2 teaspoons coconut sugar (optional)
1 red Asian shallot, finely chopped
1 spring onion, finely chopped

Salad

120 g wombok cabbage, shredded
1 carrot, cut into matchsticks
1 handful of bean sprouts
2 handfuls of Thai basil, Vietnamese
    mint and coriander leaves
3 tablespoons olive oil
1 tablespoon apple cider vinegar
sea salt

* See Glossary

To make the marinade, place the lemongrass, coriander roots, garlic and 1 teaspoon of pepper in the bowl of a food processor and process until finely chopped. Add the sugar (if using), fish sauce and tamari and continue to process to a paste.

Transfer the marinade to a container, add the pork fillets and turn to coat in the marinade. Cover and refrigerate for at least 2 hours or overnight for best results.

To make the nam jim jaew, combine the tamarind and 1 ½ tablespoons of water in a small bowl and stir until dissolved. Strain the mixture into another small bowl and discard the solids. Using a mortar and pestle, pound the chilli and garlic to a fine paste. Add the remaining ingredients and stir well. Adjust the seasoning if necessary – it should taste hot, sour and salty.

Preheat a chargrill pan over medium–high heat. Remove the pork from the marinade, reserving the marinade. Drizzle a little coconut oil or fat over the pork and cook, turning occasionally and basting with the reserved marinade, for about 15 minutes, or until browned all over and just cooked through. Transfer the pork to a plate, cover loosely with foil and rest for 5 minutes.

Place all the salad ingredients in a bowl and mix to combine. Season with salt and pepper.

Thickly slice the pork and serve with the nam jim jaew, salad and lime cheeks on the side.

I believe red meat is one of the most important superfoods on the planet. Organic beef from free-range, pasture-fed and -finished cattle provides protein and invaluable nutrients such as iron, zinc, vitamin B12 and omega-3 fats, which are essential for heart and brain health. Here is a simple, tasty and incredibly easy recipe that the whole family will enjoy.

SIMPLE SIRLOIN WITH HERB SALAD

SERVES 4

4 x 160 g sirloin steaks
2 tablespoons coconut oil or
    good-quality animal fat*
sea salt and freshly ground
    black pepper

Dressing
2 tablespoons lemon juice
3 tablespoons extra-virgin olive oil
1 garlic clove, finely grated
1 teaspoon finely chopped
    rosemary leaves

Herb salad
2 handfuls of flat-leaf parsley leaves
1 handful of chervil leaves
1 small handful of chives,
    snipped into 4 cm lengths
2 handfuls of mixed salad leaves
4 radishes, thinly sliced

Mustard aioli
100 g Mayonnaise (page 201)
1 tablespoon Dijon mustard
4 Garlic Confit cloves (page 199),
    crushed

* See Glossary

Heat a barbecue grill plate to hot or a large chargrill pan over high heat.

Brush the steaks with the coconut oil or fat and season with salt and pepper. Cook the steaks on one side for 3 minutes, or until golden, then flip and cook the other side for 3 minutes for medium–rare. Place the steaks on a plate, loosely cover with a cloth and rest for 4–6 minutes, keeping warm.

Place all the dressing ingredients in a bowl and whisk to combine. Season with salt and pepper to taste.

Place all the herb salad ingredients in a large bowl, pour in only enough dressing to coat the leaves and gently toss.

To make the mustard aioli, mix the mayonnaise, mustard and garlic confit together and season with salt and pepper if needed.

Spoon the remaining dressing over the steak, if desired, and serve with the salad and mustard aioli.

Per Serve: Total carbs: 5 g | Net carbs: 3 g | Fat: 45 g | Protein: 50 g | Fat 65% | Protein 33% | Carbs 2%

These Greek-style lamb skewers have a lot of flavour and are a wonderful addition to your weeknight keto menu as they are so easy to prepare.

LAMB SKEWERS WITH CUMIN AND CHILLI

SERVES 4

500 g lamb mince
100 g lamb or pork fat, minced
   (ask your butcher)
2 garlic cloves, finely chopped
1½ teaspoons ground cumin
1½ teaspoons dried mint
2 teaspoons dried oregano
½ teaspoon chilli flakes
2 teaspoons pomegranate molasses*,
   plus extra to serve
sea salt and freshly ground
   black pepper
olive oil, for brushing

Salad

1 fennel bulb, thinly sliced using
   a mandoline
1 large handful of mint leaves
1 tablespoon lemon juice
2 tablespoons extra-virgin olive oil

To serve

oregano leaves
Tzatziki (page 98)
lemon wedges

* See Glossary

Soak eight bamboo skewers in cold water for 20 minutes (or use metal skewers). Drain.

Combine the lamb, lamb or pork fat, garlic, cumin, dried mint and oregano, chilli flakes, pomegranate molasses and some salt and pepper in a bowl and mix thoroughly.

Divide the lamb mixture into eight portions, then shape each portion around a skewer. Place the skewers on a tray, cover and refrigerate for 30 minutes.

To make the salad, place the fennel and mint in a bowl, pour over the lemon juice and olive oil and toss gently. Season with salt and pepper.

Heat a barbecue hotplate to medium and brush with a little olive oil. Add the skewers and cook for 3½ minutes, then turn and cook for a further 3½ minutes, or until cooked through.

Arrange the skewers on a platter, scatter over the oregano leaves and serve with the salad, tzatziki and lemon wedges. If you like, you can drizzle a little more pomegranate molasses over the skewers.

Per Serve: Total carbs: 13 g | Net carbs: 9 g | Fat: 38 g | Protein: 34 g | Fat 65% | Protein 26% | Carbs 9%

This is a favourite in our household when we want something super quick and delicious. My daughters love chimichurri and I encourage you to try it, as introducing a broader range of ingredients and flavours to even the fussiest of eaters helps to open up picky palates. Duck fat–roasted cabbage, sautéed spinach or any other vegetable that takes your fancy will work well here. We love a drizzle of red wine jus with our steak and I often make up a cup or two when I make beef bone broth, then freeze it in small portions so we always have some on hand. It's delicious served with a green salad on the side.

MINUTE STEAK WITH CHIMICHURRI AND MUSHROOMS

SERVES 4

80 ml (⅓ cup) coconut oil or
    good-quality animal fat*
250 g Swiss brown mushrooms
    (or mushrooms of your
    choice), sliced
2 garlic cloves, finely chopped
8 x 70–80 g minute steaks

Chimichurri
4 garlic cloves, peeled
sea salt
1–2 pinches of chilli flakes, plus extra
    to serve (optional)
2 very large handfuls of flat-leaf
    parsley leaves
2 very large handfuls of
    coriander leaves
80 ml (⅓ cup) apple cider vinegar
1 teaspoon ground cumin
250 ml (1 cup) olive oil
freshly ground black pepper

* See Glossary

To make the chimichurri, place the garlic and a little salt in a mortar and crush with the pestle. Add the chilli flakes, parsley and coriander and pound to a paste. Stir in the vinegar, cumin and olive oil, then taste and season with salt and pepper. Alternatively, place all the ingredients in a blender and blend to a paste. Set aside.

Heat 2 tablespoons of the coconut oil or fat in a frying pan over medium–high heat. Add the mushroom and sauté for 2–4 minutes until tender. Add the garlic and cook for 30–60 seconds until fragrant and starting to colour. Season with salt and pepper. Set aside and cover to keep warm.

Heat a barbecue hotplate to hot. Brush the steaks with the remaining coconut oil or fat and season with salt and pepper. Cook for 1–2 minutes on each side, or until cooked to your liking.

Serve the steaks and mushrooms on a platter, drizzle over the chimichurri and sprinkle with extra chilli flakes, if desired.

Searching for a delicious keto dish that keeps on giving? Look no further. Cooking a meal like this – which, by the way, is perfect for dinner parties – generally means you'll have leftovers. To me, any leftovers are just as good, if not better, as when the lamb comes out of the oven. You could add eggs and greens for breakfast, toss with a salad for lunch or stir into a broth with vegetables for an unforgettable dinner. This lamb also works a treat served with cauliflower hummus (page 194), coconut yoghurt (page 196) and roasted low-carb veggies.

MIDDLE EASTERN LAMB SHOULDER

SERVES 6

4 garlic cloves, chopped
1 handful of mint leaves, chopped,
    plus extra leaves to serve
1 handful of coriander leaves, chopped
3 tablespoons orange juice
zest and juice of 1 lemon
½ teaspoon orange zest
3 tablespoons melted coconut
    oil or good-quality animal fat*,
    plus extra for greasing
sea salt and freshly ground
    black pepper
2 onions, sliced
1 x 1.5 kg lamb shoulder, bone in
500 ml (2 cups) Chicken Bone Broth
    (page 195) or lamb bone broth
1 handful of flat-leaf parsley leaves,
    to serve

Middle Eastern spice mix
1 tablespoon ground cumin
1 tablespoon ground coriander
1 tablespoon sumac
½ teaspoon ground allspice
½ teaspoon chilli flakes
½ teaspoon ground cinnamon

* See Glossary

Preheat the oven to 240°C (220°C fan-forced).

To make the spice mix, place all the ingredients in a bowl and mix to combine.

Place the garlic, mint and coriander leaves in the bowl of a food processor and blend until finely chopped. With the motor running, add the orange and lemon juices and zests and 3 tablespoons of water. Blend to form a wet paste. Add the spice mix and coconut oil or fat and pulse a few times to combine. Season with salt and pepper.

Using the tip of a sharp knife, make incisions to a depth of 5 mm all over the lamb.

Scatter the onion into the base of a large roasting tin. Sit the lamb on top and rub the spice paste evenly over the surface of the lamb. Season with salt and pepper.

Pour half the broth into the bowl of the food processor and stir to remove any remaining spice paste from the base and side, then pour the liquid into the tin along with the remaining broth.

Roast the lamb for 30 minutes, or until well browned, basting the meat occasionally with the cooking juices. Reduce the temperature to 140°C (120°C fan-forced), tightly cover the tin with foil and braise for 5–6 hours until the meat is tender and falling off the bone. Rest for 10 minutes, then scatter the mint and parsley over the lamb and serve.

Per Serve: Total carbs: 11 g | Net carbs: 8 g | Fat: 47 g | Protein: 111 g | Fat 46% | Protein 50% | Carbs 4%

VEGGIE

SIDES

This beautiful and nutritious salad is simply the best. Using a combination of fresh herbs and adding a very simple dressing to gently coat each leaf makes every mouthful utterly delicious. You can, of course, add watercress, lettuce or spinach leaves to bulk out your salad, and nuts and seeds are optional.

HERB WELLNESS BOWL

SERVES 4

1 handful of dill fronds
1 handful of flat-leaf parsley leaves
1 handful of coriander leaves
1 handful of chervil leaves
1 handful of basil leaves
1 handful of mint leaves
1 handful of chives, snipped
300 g savoy cabbage, shredded

Almond dressing

1 teaspoon finely chopped
    tarragon leaves
1 teaspoon Dijon mustard
zest and juice of 1 large lemon
3 tablespoons extra-virgin olive oil
70 g almonds, toasted and chopped
sea salt and freshly ground
    black pepper

To make the dressing, place the tarragon, mustard and lemon zest and juice in a small bowl and whisk. Slowly whisk in the olive oil until well combined, then stir in the almonds. Season with salt and pepper.

To assemble the salad, place the herbs and cabbage in a large bowl. Drizzle on the dressing and gently toss to coat. Season with more salt and pepper, if needed.

NOTE

You could replace the lemon zest and juice in the dressing with 2 tablespoons of vinegar: try apple cider vinegar or white or red wine vinegar.

Tonnato sauce – mayonnaise blended with tuna – is an Italian classic that is usually served over slow-cooked veal. I wanted to take that approach and give it a Japanese makeover. Here, I have added furikake seasoning and bonito flakes, which introduce a lovely umami flavour to the dish.

PAN-FRIED BROCCOLINI WITH TONNATO SAUCE

SERVES 4

2 tablespoons coconut oil or
   good-quality animal fat*
2 bunches of broccolini
   (about 300 g)
1 tablespoon Furikake Seasoning
   (page 198)
a good pinch of bonito flakes*

Tonnato sauce
80 g jarred tuna*, in brine or olive oil
2 salted anchovy fillets, rinsed
   and patted dry
125 g (½ cup) Aioli (page 192)
1 teaspoon lemon juice
sea salt and freshly ground
   black pepper

* See Glossary

To make the tonnato sauce, place the tuna, anchovies, aioli and lemon juice in the bowl of a food processor and blend until smooth. Season with salt and pepper, if needed. Set aside.

Heat the coconut oil or fat in a frying pan over medium heat. Add the broccolini and 2 tablespoons of water and sauté for 7–8 minutes until the broccolini is cooked through and lightly golden. Season with salt and pepper.

To serve, spread 3 tablespoons of tonnato sauce on each serving plate. Place some broccolini on the sauce, then sprinkle the furikake and bonito flakes over the top.

TIP
Leftover tonnato sauce can be stored in an airtight container in the fridge for 3–5 days.

Per Serve: Total carbs: 9 g | Net carbs: 2 g | Fat: 36 g | Protein: 9 g | Fat 81% | Protein 10% | Carbs 9%

Sometimes a simple salad with just a few leaves and a vegetable is all you need to accompany a rich or delicate meal. The lovely aniseed flavour of fennel works well with seafood, pork, steak, duck, chicken and game.

KALE AND FENNEL SALAD

SERVES 6

1 bunch of purple kale (about 300 g), stems discarded and leaves torn
1 tablespoon olive oil
1 fennel bulb, trimmed
1 granny smith apple, core removed
1 handful of flat-leaf parsley leaves
1 handful of dill fronds
1 handful of basil leaves

Dressing
1 tablespoon wholegrain mustard
2 tablespoons lemon juice or apple cider vinegar
zest of 1 lemon
1 teaspoon maple syrup or honey (optional)
80 ml (⅓ cup) extra-virgin olive oil
sea salt and freshly ground black pepper

To make the dressing, place the mustard, lemon juice or vinegar, lemon zest and maple syrup or honey (if using) in a small bowl and whisk together. Slowly whisk in the olive oil until well combined. Season with salt and pepper, to taste.

Place the kale in a large bowl and pour over the olive oil. Rub the oil into the leaves with your hands (this removes the waxy coating and allows the leaves to absorb the dressing). Set aside.

Using a mandoline or vegetable peeler, thinly slice the fennel and apple, then place in the bowl with the kale.

When ready to serve, gently toss the salad with the herbs and dressing. Arrange on plates or a large platter and serve.

Per Serve: Total carbs: 13 g | Net carbs: 9 g | Fat: 15 g | Protein: 3 g | Fat 70% | Protein 5% | Carbs 25%

Asparagus is a great prebiotic and when it's in season I can't get enough of it. This very simple preparation doesn't overshadow the unique flavour of asparagus and makes for a welcome side to eggs, meat and seafood. If asparagus isn't available, then use silverbeet, bok choy, broccoli, mushrooms, okra or green beans.

CHARGRILLED ASPARAGUS WITH GARLIC AND LEMON DRESSING

SERVES 6

2 tablespoons coconut oil or
    good-quality animal fat*,
    plus extra for brushing
3 bunches of asparagus (about
    660 g), trimmed
sea salt and freshly ground
    black pepper
8 garlic cloves, thinly sliced
3 tablespoons chopped flat-leaf
    parsley leaves
finely grated zest and juice of 1 lemon
3 tablespoons olive oil

* See Glossary

Heat a large chargrill pan over medium–high heat. Brush the pan with a little coconut oil or fat, add the asparagus in batches and cook for 1–2 minutes until charred on all sides. Season with salt and pepper. Set aside.

Heat the coconut oil or fat in a large frying pan over medium heat, add the garlic and cook for 1 minute, or until it just starts to colour.

Add the asparagus and parsley to the pan and cook, tossing, for about 30 seconds, or until the asparagus is cooked through but still slightly crisp in the middle. Remove from the heat, add the lemon juice and olive oil and give the pan another good toss. Season with salt and pepper, if needed.

Arrange the asparagus in a serving dish, spoon on the garlic and lemon dressing and sprinkle over the lemon zest to finish.

We have a wonderful veggie garden at our farm and always have greens growing, so every mealtime we go out and harvest some for the table. This is a recipe we often use. It is so easy and yummy and almost any green veggie you can think of will be perfectly at home with the bone broth and garlicky dressing.

GARLICKY BRAISED GREENS

SERVES 4

400 ml Chicken Bone Broth
    (page 195)
6 silverbeet stems, leaves and stems
    separated and cut into 8 cm
    lengths
½ bunch of kale (about 150 g), stems
    discarded and leaves torn
1 bunch of English spinach (about
    200 g), stems removed
sea salt and freshly ground
    black pepper
80 ml (⅓ cup) good-quality
    animal fat*
5 garlic cloves, thinly sliced
2 teaspoons lemon juice

* See Glossary

Pour the chicken broth into a large saucepan and bring to a simmer over medium heat. Add the silverbeet stems, reduce the heat to medium–low and simmer for 5 minutes. Next, add the kale, silverbeet leaves and spinach, cover with a lid, and cook for 5–6 minutes until the leaves are wilted. Season with salt and pepper.

Meanwhile, in a frying pan over medium heat, gently heat the fat, then add the garlic and cook for about 1–2 minutes, or until it just starts to colour. Remove from the heat, add the lemon juice and stir through.

When the greens are ready, pour over the garlic dressing, season with some more salt and pepper, if needed, and serve immediately.

Per Serve: Total carbs: 7 g | Net carbs: 5 g | Fat: 21 g | Protein: 5 g | Fat 82% | Protein 8% | Carbs 10%

We try to feature greens at most meals in one way or another, so I am always experimenting to make them unique and fun to eat. This side dish works beautifully with smoked trout, flaked eel, grilled fish, steak or spiced roast chicken. Fold through some kraut, kimchi or pickles to add a little probiotic goodness.

BROCCOLINI AND DAIKON WITH MISO DRESSING

SERVES 4

2 tablespoons coconut oil or
   good-quality animal fat*
2 bunches of broccolini (about
   300 g), trimmed
sea salt and freshly ground
   black pepper
1 bunch of English spinach (about
   200 g), stems removed
200 g daikon, cut into matchsticks
3 tablespoons Typhoon Garlic
   (page 205)
1 toasted nori* sheet, torn
2 teaspoons toasted sesame seeds
1 small handful of baby shiso leaves
   or coriander leaves

Miso dressing
2 tablespoons apple cider vinegar
2 tablespoons shiro miso
1 tablespoon tamari
3 tablespoons olive oil
1 teaspoon toasted sesame oil
1 tablespoon finely grated ginger

* See Glossary

Heat 1 tablespoon of the coconut oil or fat in a large frying pan over medium heat. Add the broccolini and 3 tablespoons of water and sauté for 5 minutes, or until slightly golden and tender. Transfer to a plate and season with salt and pepper.

Heat the remaining coconut oil or fat in the same pan, then add the spinach and sauté for 2 minutes, or until wilted. Season with salt and pepper.

Combine all the miso dressing ingredients with 1 tablespoon of water in a small bowl and whisk until smooth.

Place the broccolini, spinach and daikon on a serving platter and gently toss. Scatter over the typhoon garlic, nori, sesame seeds and shiso or coriander leaves. Drizzle over the miso dressing and serve.

Per Serve: Total carbs: 15 g | Net carbs: 10 g | Fat: 20 g | Protein: 6 g | Fat 71% | Protein 8% | Carbs 21%

When summer comes around and cucumbers are cheap and plentiful, try this salad. It's refreshing, light and super tasty, with the added richness of the creamy green goddess dressing, and it makes the perfect accompaniment to any of the meals in this book. You could easily turn this into a complete meal with the addition of wild salmon, smoked fish, steak or soft-boiled eggs.

CUCUMBER, RADISH AND HERB SALAD WITH GREEN GODDESS DRESSING

SERVES 4

2 small Lebanese cucumbers, cut into matchsticks
1 large handful of watercress sprigs
1 handful of mint leaves
1 handful of chervil leaves
1 handful of flat-leaf parsley leaves
5 radishes, thinly sliced

Green goddess dressing

1 avocado
90 g (⅓ cup) Coconut Yoghurt (page 196)
3 tablespoons lemon juice
1 garlic clove, finely chopped
2 teaspoons finely chopped salted anchovy fillets
1 handful of flat-leaf parsley leaves
3 tablespoons chopped coriander leaves
1 tablespoon chopped tarragon leaves
pinch of sea salt
80 ml (⅓ cup) olive oil

Mustard dressing

1 teaspoon wholegrain mustard
3 teaspoons apple cider vinegar
2 tablespoons extra-virgin olive oil
freshly ground black pepper

To make the green goddess dressing, place all the ingredients except the oil in the bowl of a food processor and process until well combined. With the motor running, slowly pour in the oil and whiz until the dressing thickens and the herbs are finely chopped.

To make the mustard dressing, place the mustard, vinegar and olive oil in a bowl and whisk until well combined. Season with salt and pepper.

To assemble the salad, arrange the cucumber, watercress, herbs and radish on a serving platter. Drizzle over the mustard dressing, dollop on the green goddess dressing and season with salt and pepper, if desired.

HIGH-
DAY

CARB

The humble and delicious quiche has got to be one of the most popular dishes ever. When it comes to family food it ticks so many boxes: it is cheap, quick, easy and everyone loves it. My quiche replaces the pastry with sweet potato, which adds more nutrition and a tonne of flavour. Keep in mind that too much sweet potato can bring you out of ketosis, so enjoy this recipe when you want more healthy carbs. This makes a wonderful school or work lunch.

HAM AND VEGGIE QUICHE

SERVES 6

2 tablespoons melted coconut oil
   or good-quality animal fat*,
   plus extra for greasing
2 sweet potatoes (about 700 g in
   total), peeled and thinly sliced

Filling
1 tablespoon coconut oil or
   good-quality animal fat*
200 g ham, sliced
½ onion, chopped
1 leek, white part only, chopped
3 garlic cloves, finely chopped
1 large handful of baby spinach leaves
sea salt and freshly ground
   black pepper
4 eggs
250 ml (1 cup) coconut cream
2½ tablespoons Chicken Bone Broth
   (page 195)
pinch of freshly grated nutmeg

* See Glossary

Preheat the oven to 200°C (180°C fan-forced). Grease a 23 cm round tart tin with coconut oil or fat.

Place the slices of sweet potato in the prepared tin, slightly overlapping them in a fan-shaped circle to completely cover the base. When it's time to do the side, cut the slices into half-moon shapes, then fan around the side, cut-side down, making sure there are no gaps.

Gently brush the sweet potato base with the coconut oil or fat and bake for 20 minutes, or until just tender. Remove from the oven and set aside until needed.

Meanwhile, to start on the filling, heat the oil or fat in a large frying pan over medium–high heat. Add the ham and fry for 3–5 minutes until lightly golden. Remove from the pan and set aside until needed.

Using the same pan and the oil or fat left over from cooking the ham, sauté the onion over medium heat for 5 minutes, or until translucent. Add the leek and garlic and cook for 2 minutes to soften. Remove from the heat, return the ham to the pan, add the spinach and give everything a good stir. Season with salt and pepper.

Crack the eggs into a bowl, then pour in the coconut cream and broth and whisk until smooth. Mix in the nutmeg and season with salt and pepper.

Spoon the sautéed veg and ham mixture onto the sweet potato crust and spread out to form an even layer, then slowly pour over the egg mixture. Bake for 20–25 minutes until the egg is set and golden on top. Allow to rest for 5 minutes before cutting.

These sweet potato toasts are a lot of fun and are super easy to make. You can use your toaster (they might need a few turns to get them nice and crispy) or you can pan-fry or roast them until golden and cooked through. From there, simply add your toppings. Have a play and see what you love to add.

SWEET POTATO TOASTS WITH BACON AND AVO

SERVES 4 AS A SNACK

1 large sweet potato, cut into 5 mm
    thick slices
1 tablespoon melted coconut oil or
    good-quality animal fat*
sea salt and freshly ground
    black pepper
lemon wedges, to serve

Topping
4 rindless bacon rashers, chopped
2 avocados
2 teaspoons extra-virgin olive oil
3 teaspoons lime juice, or more
    to taste
3 tablespoons salmon roe
micro herbs, to serve

* See Glossary

Preheat the oven to 230°C (210°C fan-forced). Line two baking trays with baking paper.

Place the sweet potato in a single layer on one prepared tray and lightly brush both sides with the coconut oil or fat. Sprinkle on some salt and pepper, then bake for 10 minutes, or until tender.

Preheat the oven grill to high.

Remove the paper from the tray with the cooked sweet potato and grill the sweet potato for 1–1½ minutes on each side, or until golden and crispy.

Reduce the oven to 200°C (180°C fan-forced).

Meanwhile, start on the topping. Spread the bacon in a single layer on the remaining prepared tray and bake for 12–15 minutes until golden and crisp. Transfer to a serving bowl and set aside, keeping warm until needed.

Mash the avocados in a bowl. Add the olive oil and lime juice and gently mix with a spoon. Taste, add more lime juice if desired and season with salt and pepper.

To serve, spoon some avocado onto the sweet potato toasts, then top with the salmon roe or bacon (or both) and scatter over the micro herbs. Serve with lemon wedges for squeezing over.

Per Serve: Total carbs: 15 g | Net carbs: 9 g | Fat: 19 g | Protein: 6 g | Fat 68% | Protein 10% | Carbs 22%

When the weather becomes cold I turn to warm, nourishing, slow-cooked soups, braises and roasts. This comforting seafood chowder, perfect for when you want to break out of ketosis, will warm your tummy and the cockles of your heart. To keep it keto and retain the essence of the dish, simply omit the sweet potato and add some spinach or watercress at the end of cooking to lighten it up.

SEAFOOD CHOWDER

SERVES 4

1½ tablespoons coconut oil or
    good-quality animal fat*
200 g rindless bacon rashers, diced
2 carrots, diced
2 celery stalks, diced
1 onion, chopped
3 garlic cloves, finely chopped
1 turnip, diced
1 small sweet potato, diced
1 litre Fish or Chicken Bone Broth
    (page 198 or 195)
250 ml (1 cup) coconut cream
1 bay leaf and 4 thyme sprigs, tied
    into a bundle
500 g mussels, scrubbed and
    debearded
300 g white fish fillets (such
    as snapper), chopped into
    bite-sized pieces
150 g scallop meat, roughly chopped
200 g roughly chopped, peeled and
    deveined raw prawns
sea salt and freshly ground
    black pepper
1 tablespoon chopped flat-leaf
    parsley leaves
lemon wedges, to serve

* See Glossary

Heat 2 teaspoons of the coconut oil or fat in a large saucepan over medium heat. Add the bacon and cook for 6–8 minutes until golden and crisp. Remove the bacon from the pan, reserving the oil. Place the bacon on a plate and set aside until needed.

Return the pan to medium heat, add the remaining coconut oil or fat, the carrot, celery and onion and cook for 10 minutes, or until the onion is softened. Add the garlic and cook for 30 seconds, or until fragrant. Add the turnip and sweet potato and cook, stirring occasionally, for 5 minutes. Pour in the broth and coconut cream, add the herb bundle, then reduce the heat to medium–low and simmer for 20 minutes, or until the veggies are tender. Add the mussels, cover with a lid and cook for 4 minutes, or until all the mussels open. Using tongs, remove the mussels from the pan and set aside.

Carefully transfer half the stock and veggies to a blender. Blend until smooth, then return to the pan. Stir well, then add the fish and scallop meat and stir again. Cook for a further 5 minutes.

Meanwhile, remove the mussels from their shells and roughly chop the meat. Add the mussel meat and prawns to the chowder, stir well and cook for a further minute until all the seafood is cooked through. Remove the herb bundle and season with salt and pepper.

Just before serving, stir in the bacon and parsley. Serve with lemon wedges for squeezing over.

Katsu – a Japanese curry sauce that is served alongside crumbed meats – is a flavour bomb that will have you rethinking the humble schnitzel. It is also awesome over grilled vegetables or fried eggs.

JAPANESE CRUMBED CHICKEN WITH KATSU

SERVES 4

4 boneless chicken thighs, skin on
150 g (1½ cups) almond meal
3 tablespoons tapioca flour*
2 eggs
80 ml (⅓ cup) coconut milk
coconut oil or good-quality animal
  fat*, for shallow-frying
80 g (⅓ cup) Japanese Mayonnaise
  (page 199)

Katsu

1 tablespoon coconut oil
1 onion, finely chopped
2 garlic cloves, grated
1 tablespoon finely grated ginger
sea salt
1½ tablespoons mild curry powder
1½ tablespoons tomato paste
1 tablespoon tamari
1 tablespoon honey (optional)
350 ml Chicken Bone Broth
  (page 195)
400 ml coconut milk
freshly ground black pepper
1 tablespoon tapioca flour, if needed

Salad

200 g savoy cabbage
200 g daikon, cut into matchsticks
3 spring onions, cut into matchsticks
1 handful of sprouts (broccoli or alfalfa)
4 shiso or baby cos leaves, shredded
baby shiso leaves (optional)

Dressing

3 tablespoons olive oil
1½ tablespoons lemon juice
1 teaspoon tamari

* See Glossary

To make the katsu, heat the oil in a large saucepan over medium heat. Add the onion, garlic, ginger and a pinch of salt and cook, stirring, for 5 minutes, or until the onion is softened. Stir in the curry powder, tomato paste, tamari and honey (if using). Slowly pour in the broth and coconut milk, then whisk until smooth and combined. Season with salt and pepper. Bring to the boil, reduce the heat to low, and simmer for 30 minutes until thickened. If the sauce is too thin, mix the tapioca flour with 2 tablespoons of cold water and stir in to thicken.

Meanwhile, place the chicken thighs between two sheets of baking paper and pound with a meat mallet until about 1 cm thick. Place the almond meal in a shallow bowl, season with a little salt and pepper and mix well. Place the tapioca flour in another shallow bowl. In a third bowl, whisk the eggs and coconut milk until combined. Working with one piece at a time, dust the pounded chicken in the tapioca flour, shake off any excess, then dip in the egg mixture and evenly coat in the almond meal.

Heat the coconut oil or fat in a large, deep frying pan over medium–high heat until about 160°C. (To test, place a tiny piece of chicken in the hot oil – if it immediately starts to bubble around the chicken, the oil is ready.) Add the chicken in batches and fry for 4–5 minutes on each side until golden and cooked through. Remove from the pan and drain on paper towel. Season with salt and pepper.

To make the salad, toss the cabbage, daikon, spring onion, sprouts and shredded shiso or cos in a bowl and season with a little salt and pepper. Arrange the salad in a serving bowl.

Combine the dressing ingredients in a small bowl. Pour the dressing over the salad and lightly toss, then scatter over the baby shiso leaves (if using).

Place the chicken on a serving platter and pour over some katsu. Spoon the mayonnaise into a serving bowl and serve on the side with the cabbage salad.

Per Serve: Total carbs: 26 g | Net carbs: 20 g | Fat: 74 g | Protein: 41 g | Fat 71% | Protein 19% | Carbs 10%

Meatballs are popular in many cultures around the world and are a dream dish for families, as everyone absolutely loves them. Here is my Mexican take on a wonderful keto-friendly dish.

MEXICAN MEATBALLS WITH CRISPY ONION RINGS

SERVES 4

2 small onions, thinly sliced into rings
tapioca flour*, for dusting
melted coconut oil or good-quality
   animal fat*, for frying

Meatballs
650 g beef mince
1 egg
2 garlic cloves, finely chopped
1 teaspoon ground cumin
½ cup finely chopped coriander leaves
½ teaspoon smoked paprika
3 tablespoons lard, softened
sea salt and freshly ground
   black pepper

Spicy Mexican sauce
2 tablespoons coconut oil or
   good-quality animal fat*
1 onion, finely chopped
1 red capsicum, chopped
80 g Swiss brown mushrooms, sliced
2 garlic cloves, finely chopped
1½ tablespoons tomato paste
1 tablespoon chipotle chillies
   in adobo sauce, chopped
1½ teaspoons smoked paprika
1½ teaspoons ground cumin
1½ teaspoons ground coriander
1½ teaspoons dried oregano
600 ml Beef Bone Broth (page 193)
200 g tomato passata

To serve
coriander leaves
sliced jalapeño chilli
Paleo Sour Cream (page 202)
lime wedges

* See Glossary

Separate the onion into rings and lightly dust in the tapioca flour. Pour the coconut oil or fat into a saucepan to a depth of 5 cm and place over medium–high heat. Add the onion rings and fry for 3–4 minutes until crisp. Drain on paper towel and set aside.

To make the meatballs, combine all the ingredients in a bowl and mix well. Roll into walnut-sized balls, then place the meatballs on a tray, cover and refrigerate for 30 minutes.

To make the spicy Mexican sauce, heat the coconut oil or fat in a large saucepan over medium heat. Add the onion and capsicum and sauté for 5 minutes, or until softened. Add the mushrooms and sauté for 2 minutes. Stir in the garlic, tomato paste, chipotle chilli and ground spices and cook for 1 minute, or until fragrant. Add the dried oregano, broth and passata, stir well and simmer over medium–low heat for 30 minutes, or until the sauce is rich and full of flavour. Season with salt and pepper.

Meanwhile, heat 1 tablespoon of coconut oil or fat in a large heavy-based frying pan over medium–high heat, add the meatballs, in batches if necessary, and fry until golden brown on all sides. Pour in the sauce, cover with a lid and cook over low heat for 6–7 minutes, until the meatballs are cooked through.

Scatter the crispy onion rings, coriander leaves and jalapeño chilli over the meatballs and serve with paleo sour cream and lime wedges on the side.

Mexican food is becoming a staple in our home. One of the things I really appreciate in this recipe is the way the chicken is elevated by the spices. Make a big batch of the Mexican-spiced chicken in these enchiladas as it comes in handy for salads and wraps. If you want to stay in ketosis, replace the coconut tortillas with lettuce or cabbage wraps or zucchini noodles. Serve with some paleo sour cream (page 202) and grated pumpkin cheese (page 203), if desired.

SPICY CHICKEN ENCHILADAS

SERVES 4

2 tablespoons coconut oil or
    good-quality animal fat*
1 onion, chopped
700 g boneless chicken thighs,
    skin on, cut into 1 cm thick strips
4 garlic cloves, finely chopped
1 red capsicum, diced
2 teaspoons thyme leaves, chopped
1 tablespoon chopped chipotle chillies
    in adobo sauce
1 teaspoon Mexican spice mix
1 teaspoon ground cumin
1 teaspoon smoked paprika
125 ml (½ cup) Chicken Bone Broth
    (page 195) or water
4 x Coconut Tortillas (page 195)
Guacamole (page 88), to serve
coriander leaves, to serve
thinly sliced spring onion, to serve

* See Glossary

Sauce

1 tablespoon coconut oil or
    good-quality animal fat*
1 onion, chopped
4 garlic cloves, chopped
1 red capsicum, chopped
1 teaspoon thyme leaves, chopped
2 tablespoons tomato paste
1 teaspoon smoked paprika
1 teaspoon ground cumin
600 g whole peeled tomatoes,
    crushed (see Note page 163)
400 ml Chicken Bone Broth
    (page 195)
1 tablespoon pickled jalapeño chillies,
    chopped, plus extra to serve
2 tablespoons washed and finely
    chopped coriander roots, stalks
    and leaves
2 teaspoons chopped chipotle chillies
    in adobo sauce
1 tablespoon extra-virgin olive oil
sea salt and freshly ground
    black pepper

Recipe continued over the page

To make the sauce, heat the coconut oil or fat in a large saucepan over medium heat. Add the onion and cook for 5 minutes, or until translucent. Add the garlic, capsicum, thyme, tomato paste and spices and sauté for 30 seconds, or until fragrant. Stir in the tomatoes, broth, jalapeño, chopped coriander and chipotle chillies and bring to a simmer. Reduce the heat to low and cook for 1½ hours to allow the flavours to fully develop. Add some water if the sauce starts to dry out. Remove from the heat and stir through the olive oil. Using a hand-held blender, pulse a few times until the sauce is blended but still slightly chunky. Season with salt and pepper.

Heat the coconut oil or fat in a large frying pan over medium heat. Add the onion and cook for 5 minutes, or until softened. Add the chicken, garlic, capsicum and thyme and cook for 5 minutes, then add the chipotle chillies, Mexican spice, cumin and paprika and cook for 2 minutes, or until fragrant. Pour in the broth or water, stir well and cook for 10 minutes, or until the chicken is cooked through.

Preheat the oven to 220°C (200°C fan-forced).

To assemble the enchiladas, place the tortillas on a chopping board and top with the chicken mixture. Fold over the ends of the tortillas and roll up to seal. Spoon 250 ml of the sauce into the base of a large baking dish, then carefully place the enchiladas, seam-side down, in the dish. Spoon the remaining sauce over the middle of the enchiladas. Bake for 15–20 minutes until the edges are golden.

Top the enchiladas with the guacamole, extra jalapeño, coriander leaves and spring onion and serve.

NOTE

I prefer to buy diced and whole peeled tomatoes in jars rather than cans, due to the presence of Bisphenol A (BPA) in some cans. BPA is a toxic chemical that can interfere with our hormonal system.

This is my healthier version of the much-loved family classic. I use layers of sweet potato instead of pasta sheets, but you can easily try slices of zucchini for a lower carb option if you want to stay in ketosis. Serve with a side of salad and some cultured veggies.

CURRIED LASAGNE

SERVES 8

3 large sweet potatoes (about 1.2 kg), thinly sliced

80 ml (⅓ cup) melted coconut oil or good-quality animal fat*, plus extra for greasing

1 onion, chopped

1 carrot, finely chopped

1 celery stalk, finely chopped

4 garlic cloves, finely chopped

2 teaspoons brown or yellow mustard seeds

1 tablespoon garam masala

3½ teaspoons ground coriander

3½ teaspoons ground cumin

1½ teaspoons ground cardamom

1½ teaspoons ground ginger

3½ teaspoons ground turmeric

20 fresh curry leaves

800 g beef mince

600 ml Beef or Chicken Bone Broth (page 193 or 195)

400 ml coconut cream

1½ tablespoons tapioca flour mixed with 1½ tablespoons water

1 tablespoon lemon juice

sea salt and freshly ground black pepper

9 eggs

* See Glossary

Preheat the oven to 230°C (210°C fan-forced). Line two baking trays with baking paper. Grease a 2 litre casserole dish with coconut oil or fat.

Place the slices of sweet potato on the prepared trays, brush with 2 tablespoons of the coconut oil or fat and bake for 10 minutes, or until lightly golden around the edges.

Meanwhile, heat 1 tablespoon of the coconut oil or fat in a large frying pan over medium heat. Add the onion, carrot and celery and cook, stirring occasionally, for 5 minutes, or until the veggies are starting to colour. Add the garlic and mustard seeds and cook for 1 minute. Stir in the spices and curry leaves and cook for a further 30 seconds, or until fragrant. Add the mince and cook, breaking up any lumps with a wooden spoon, for 5–7 minutes. Pour in the broth and coconut cream. Reduce the heat to medium–low and bring to a gentle simmer. Cook, stirring occasionally, for 30 minutes. Add the tapioca mixture and stir until the sauce thickens. Stir in the lemon juice and season with salt and pepper.

Crack the eggs into a bowl, whisk and season with a pinch of salt and pepper. Set aside 2 tablespoons of the egg. Heat 1 teaspoon of the coconut oil or fat in a 25 cm non-stick frying pan over medium heat. Pour in one-quarter of the egg and swirl the pan to coat the base with the egg. Cook for 40–60 seconds until the egg is lightly golden underneath. Slide the omelette out of the pan and onto a cutting board. Repeat with the remaining coconut oil and egg to form four omelettes. Set aside.

Reduce the oven to 200°C (180°C fan-forced).

Cover the base of the prepared dish with a layer of sweet potato, follow with an omelette and a layer of meat sauce. Repeat this layering process, finishing with a layer of sweet potato. Lightly brush the top with the reserved egg and bake for 25 minutes, or until golden. Serve.

This is a family favourite that my daughters often request. To reduce the carbs and stay in ketosis, simply replace the sweet potato with zucchini noodles or lettuce cups.

LOADED SWEET POTATO FRIES

SERVES 4

3 large sweet potatoes (about 1.2 kg),
  cut into 1 cm thick batons
3 tablespoons tapioca flour*
600 ml melted coconut oil or
  good-quality animal fat*
sea salt
½ red onion, cut into 8 wedges
80 ml (⅓ cup) red wine vinegar
1 teaspoon honey

Jalapeño mayonnaise
1 tablespoon pickled jalapeño chillies,
  finely chopped, plus extra to serve
100 g Mayonnaise (page 201)
freshly ground black pepper
extra-virgin olive oil, for drizzling

Spicy Mexican beef
2 tablespoons coconut oil or
  good-quality animal fat*
1 onion, finely chopped
2 garlic cloves, finely chopped
1 long red chilli, halved, deseeded
  and chopped
500 g beef mince
1 teaspoon chopped chipotle chillies
  in adobo sauce
2 teaspoons smoked paprika
2 teaspoons ground cumin
1 teaspoon ground coriander
1½ tablespoons tomato paste
400 g diced tomatoes (see Note
  page 163)

To serve
Guacamole (page 88)
coriander sprigs
lime wedges

* See Glossary

Dust the sweet potato with the tapioca flour. Heat the coconut oil or fat in a large saucepan to 160°C. (To test the temperature, add a piece of sweet potato. If bubbles appear at the edges, the oil is ready.) Working in three batches, add the sweet potato and cook for 3 minutes. Drain in a single layer on paper towel, then chill in the fridge for 1 hour or in the freezer for 15 minutes. Separate the fries after chilling and before deep-frying a second time. Reheat the oil to 180°C. (To check the temperature, place a piece of sweet potato in the oil. If it bubbles vigorously, the oil is ready.) Again, working in three batches, deep-fry the sweet potato for 2–2½ minutes until golden and crisp. Drain on paper towel and season with salt. (Strain the oil and store in an airtight container in the fridge to be re-used.)

Place the red onion, vinegar and honey in a small saucepan and bring to a simmer over medium heat. Cover and cook for 1 minute, then remove from the heat and allow to cool.

To make the jalapeño mayonnaise, combine the jalapeño and mayonnaise in a bowl and mix well. Season with salt and pepper, if needed, and drizzle over the olive oil.

To make the Mexican beef, heat the coconut oil or fat in a large frying pan over medium heat. Add the onion and cook for 5 minutes, or until translucent. Stir in the garlic and chilli and cook for 1 minute. Add the beef and cook, stirring to break up any lumps, for 6 minutes, or until browned. Add the chipotle chillies, spices and tomato paste and cook for 1 minute, then stir in the tomatoes. Reduce the heat to low and simmer for 10–12 minutes, adding a little water if the sauce becomes too dry. Season with salt and pepper.

Pile the fries onto plates, top with the mince, guacamole and jalapeño mayo. Sprinkle over the coriander, red onion and extra jalapeño and serve with the lime wedges.

TIP
You could also simply coat the sweet potato in coconut oil or fat, roast in the oven until tender and top accordingly.

You might be surprised to learn that when I was 14 years old I worked at McDonald's. And I have to say it was a great gift in a work sense, as it taught me about systems, organisation, team work and cleanliness. I have put my own spin on the classic quarter pounder and used a paleo bun, organic grass-fed beef and pumpkin cheese. This burger is a great way to bring you out of ketosis. Or if you want to stay in ketosis, enjoy the patties on their own or wrapped in lettuce leaves.

PALEO 'QUARTER POUNDER'

SERVES 4

2 tablespoons coconut oil or
  good-quality animal fat*
¼ onion, finely chopped

Patties
260 g beef mince
200 g pork mince
2 tablespoons lard, melted
1 teaspoon onion powder
1 teaspoon garlic powder
½ teaspoon dried thyme
1 egg
2 teaspoons chopped flat-leaf
  parsley leaves
pinch of chilli flakes (optional)
sea salt and freshly ground
  black pepper

To serve
8 thin slices of Pumpkin Cheese
  (page 203)
4 Paleo Buns (page 201), halved
Dijon mustard
Tomato Ketchup (page 204)
dill pickles

* See Glossary

Heat 1 teaspoon of the coconut oil or fat in a frying pan over medium heat. Add the onion and cook for 3 minutes, or until softened. Remove from the heat and set aside.

Combine all the ingredients for the patties in a large bowl, mix well and season with salt and pepper. Shape into four even-sized patties.

Heat a barbecue hotplate to medium–hot or place a chargrill pan over medium–high heat. Brush with the remaining coconut oil or fat, add the patties and cook for 2–3 minutes until browned. Flip the patties and continue to cook for 2 minutes until they are browned and cooked through. Remove from the heat and keep warm.

Place a slice of pumpkin cheese on the bottom half of each burger bun and top with a patty, another slice of cheese, some onion, mustard, tomato ketchup and pickles, then top with the remaining burger bun halves. Serve.

Per Serve: Total carbs: 32 g | Net carbs: 20 g | Fat: 62 g | Protein: 46 g | Fat 66% | Protein 22% | Carbs 12%

This slow-braised lamb shoulder is one of the easiest and most delicious recipes in this book. I love to use my slow-cooker, but a flameproof casserole dish will do too; simply pop it in the oven and let the cooking process work its magic.

BRAISED LAMB SHOULDER WITH MASH

SERVES 6

1 x 1.5 kg lamb shoulder, bone in, scored with a sharp knife
2 tablespoons coconut oil or good-quality animal fat*
sea salt and freshly ground black pepper
2 onions, finely chopped
4 garlic cloves, finely chopped
2 carrots, diced
2 teaspoons finely chopped rosemary leaves
1 tablespoon ground cumin
500 ml (2 cups) Beef Bone Broth (page 193) or water, plus more if needed
400 g whole peeled tomatoes (see Note page 163)

To serve
Parsnip and Cauliflower Mash (page 202)
chopped flat-leaf parsley leaves

* See Glossary

Preheat the oven to 140°C (120°C fan-forced).

Coat the lamb with 1 tablespoon of the coconut oil or fat, then rub evenly with salt and pepper.

Heat ½ tablespoon of the coconut oil or fat in a large flameproof casserole dish over medium–high heat. Seal the lamb for 2 minutes each side, or until well browned. Remove the lamb from the dish and set aside until needed.

Reduce the heat to medium, add the remaining coconut oil or fat to the dish, then add the onion and cook, stirring occasionally, for 5–8 minutes until softened. Add the garlic, carrot and rosemary and cook for 5 minutes, or until slightly softened. Stir in the cumin and cook for 1 minute, or until fragrant. Pour in the broth and tomatoes and bring to the boil, then remove from the heat and season with salt and pepper.

Return the lamb shoulder to the dish and press down to submerge in the liquid, adding more broth or water if needed. Cover the dish with a tight-fitting lid, or tightly seal with at least two layers of foil so no steam can escape. Transfer to the oven to braise for 5½–6 hours until the meat pulls away easily from the bone. If there is any resistance, the lamb needs to be cooked for a little longer.

Carefully remove the lamb from the dish, cover with foil and set aside to rest. Place the dish over medium heat, bring the juices to a simmer and reduce for 12–15 minutes, or until it reaches a sauce consistency. Return the lamb to the dish and simmer for a further 5 minutes, or until it is heated through. Season to taste with salt and pepper.

Divide the lamb among serving plates, add a couple of big spoonfuls of mash, then ladle over the sauce and sprinkle on the parsley.

TRE

ATS

You and the kids will adore these when it is hot outside. I have loved the combination of chocolate and mint since childhood. By adding avocado, you get a delicious, rich, creamy texture and a little beef bone broth adds some gut-healing goodness. I use a high-quality edible peppermint oil, which adds a beautiful flavour; you could use fresh mint leaves instead.

CHOCOLATE, MINT AND AVOCADO POPSICLES

MAKES 8

½ avocado
4 fresh medjool dates, pitted
3 tablespoons cacao powder
350 ml coconut cream
150 ml Beef Bone Broth (page 193)
4–6 drops of edible peppermint oil,
   or to taste
1 tablespoon honey

* See Glossary

Combine all the ingredients in a high-speed blender and blend until smooth.

Pour the mixture into popsicle moulds and freeze for 2 hours. Insert a popsicle stick in the middle of each mould, then return to the freezer for 4–6 hours until frozen.

I don't have any hard and fast rules for this recipe and like to mix things up. Great-quality coconut oil, coconut butter and cacao powder are essential, but feel free to include spices and other flavourings: cayenne pepper, turmeric, ginger, cinnamon, wattleseeds, finger limes, raspberries, blueberries or Australian native bush foods work well. These treats are best kept in the fridge or freezer as the coconut oil melts quickly.

CHOC—COCONUT TREATS

MAKES 20—24

200 ml melted coconut oil, plus
    extra for greasing
350 g coconut butter, melted
80 g cacao powder
¼ teaspoon liquid stevia*, or to taste

* See Glossary

Grease a 24-hole mini muffin tray or chocolate mould tray.

Place the coconut oil, 200 g of the coconut butter, the cacao powder and stevia in a bowl and mix well. Reserve the remaining coconut butter for the filling.

Spoon half the cacao mixture evenly into the prepared holes or moulds until one-third full. Place in the fridge for 30 minutes to firm up. Remove from the fridge, spoon in the reserved coconut butter until two-thirds full, then return to the fridge to set for 10 minutes. Pour in the remaining cacao mixture and place back in the fridge to set for 30 minutes.

Tap the base of the tray on the benchtop a couple of times, then flip over to remove the chocolate treats. They should pop out easily. If they don't, try tapping the base again.

Store the treats in an airtight container in the fridge for up to 2 weeks or in the freezer for up to 3 months.

    Per Serve: Total carbs: 8 g | Net carbs: 5 g | Fat: 20 g | Protein: 2 g | Fat 86% | Protein 4% | Carbs 10%

Here, I take a very simple approach and make puddings where coconut is the star. The whole family is sure to enjoy these. If you want to reduce the carbs, simply serve the puddings without the berries or coulis.

COCONUT PUDDINGS WITH BERRIES

SERVES 4

1 tablespoon powdered gelatine*
500 ml (2 cups) coconut milk
4 egg yolks
3 tablespoons monk fruit sweetener*,
   xylitol* or erythritol*
½ teaspoon vanilla powder or
   1 teaspoon vanilla paste

To serve
fresh mixed berries
mint leaves
Berry Coulis (page 187) (optional)

* See Glossary

Place 3 tablespoons of water in a bowl and mix in the gelatine. Stand for 5 minutes to allow the gelatine granules to expand.

Meanwhile, place the coconut milk in a saucepan and bring to the boil, stirring occasionally. Remove from the heat.

In a large heatproof bowl, whisk the egg yolks, sweetener and vanilla until light and smooth. Pour in half of the hot coconut milk and whisk well. Whisk in the remaining hot coconut milk, then return the mixture to the pan. Cook over medium heat, stirring with a wooden spoon or spatula, until the mixture thickens slightly to form a custard and coats the back of the spoon. Remove from the heat and stir through the gelatine until completely dissolved. Strain through a fine sieve into a jug.

Pour the coconut custard into four small cups or ramekins, cover and transfer to the fridge to set for 2 hours.

Scatter over some berries and mint and serve, if you like, with the berry coulis.

TIP
If the mix starts to curdle after cooking, pour the mixture into a high-speed blender and blend until smooth.

Per Serve: Total carbs: 26 g | Net carbs: 24 g | Fat: 29 g | Protein: 7 g | Fat 75% | Protein 8% | Carbs 17%

For this treat, I have simply tweaked the Bounty bar – that iconic Australian snack of coconut wrapped in milk chocolate – so you can easily make your own and keep them super low carb. If you like, add a couple of drops of edible peppermint or orange oil to the coconut mixture for an extra boost of flavour.

KETO 'BOUNTY' BARS

MAKES ABOUT 20

330 g (4 cups) shredded coconut
250 ml (1 cup) coconut milk
180 ml melted coconut oil
¼ teaspoon vanilla powder or
    ½ teaspoon vanilla paste
3 tablespoons monk fruit sweetener*
    or xylitol* (you can also use
    ½ teaspoon liquid stevia*),
    or to taste
1 quantity of Keto Chocolate
    (page 184)

* See Glossary

Place the coconut in the bowl of a food processor and blitz to form crumbs. Add the coconut milk, coconut oil, vanilla and sweetener and whiz for 30 seconds to combine.

Tear a 30 x 20 cm sheet of baking paper from your roll. Place the paper on a benchtop, with the long side facing you. Working from the edge closest to you, spoon one-quarter of the coconut mixture across the sheet, leaving a 1 cm gap from the edge. Starting with the edge closest to you, begin to tightly wrap and roll all the way to the end of the paper to form a log. Smooth the outside of the log with your fingers to remove any air pockets. Gently lift and place on a tray, then repeat with the remaining mixture to create four logs. Place the logs in the fridge to set for 1 hour.

Line a tray with baking paper.

Gently melt the chocolate in a heatproof bowl over a saucepan of just-simmering water (make sure the bowl doesn't touch the water or it will overheat). Remove the coconut logs from the fridge and cut into roughly 5 cm pieces. Dip the pieces in the chocolate and place on the prepared tray. Return to the fridge for 30 minutes to set the chocolate. If the chocolate coating is quite thin, you can dip the pieces in the melted chocolate again and return to the fridge to set.

Store your 'bounty' bars in an airtight container in the fridge for up to 1 week or freeze for up to 3 months.

These are awesome to make for school fetes, P&C meetings and fundraisers. Give my ginger and turmeric cookies a shot and you and everyone who tries them will realise just how delicious keto treats can be.

GINGER AND TURMERIC COOKIES

MAKES 10

2 tablespoons coconut flour
45 g (½ cup) desiccated coconut
3 tablespoons sunflower seeds
2 tablespoons hemp seeds
2 teaspoons white chia seeds
1½ tablespoons hulled tahini
½ teaspoon bicarbonate of soda
pinch of sea salt
60 g sesame seeds
55 ml coconut oil
2 tablespoons maple syrup
50 g xylitol*
¼ teaspoon vanilla powder
½ teaspoon ground turmeric
½ teaspoon ground ginger
1 egg, lightly whisked
melted coconut butter, for drizzling
  (optional)

* See Glossary

Preheat the oven to 160°C (140°C fan-forced). Line a large baking tray with baking paper.

Place the coconut flour, desiccated coconut, sunflower seeds, hemp seeds, chia seeds, tahini, bicarbonate of soda and salt in the bowl of a food processor and blend to fine crumbs. Transfer the mixture to a bowl, stir through the sesame seeds and set aside.

Melt the coconut oil in a small saucepan over low heat, then add the maple syrup, xylitol, vanilla, turmeric and ginger. Stir to combine and bring to a simmer, then remove from the heat and set aside.

Add the egg to the coconut flour mixture and stir to combine. Pour in the coconut oil mixture and stir well until you have a soft, sticky dough.

Shape the dough into ten walnut-sized balls and gently press flat on the prepared tray, allowing space for the cookies to spread. Bake for 25 minutes, or until golden. Transfer to a wire rack to cool.

Once cool, drizzle with some melted coconut butter, if you like, or keep plain. Store in an airtight container in the pantry for up to 5 days.

Per Serve: Total carbs: 12 g | Net carbs: 9 g | Fat: 17 g | Protein: 4 g | Fat 78% | Protein 9% | Carbs 13%

Macadamias are my favourite nut and they are perfect for the keto diet as they are particularly high in healthy fats and quite low in carbs. If you don't have macadamias, you could substitute with hazelnuts, brazil nuts or almonds. Kakadu plum – also known as gubinge – is a native Australian fruit that is off-the-charts full of vitamin C.

CHOC-COATED MACADAMIA NUTS

MAKES 40

40 macadamia nuts
Kakadu plum powder (see Note) or
  ground cinnamon, for sprinkling

Keto chocolate
60 g (½ cup) cacao powder, sifted
3 tablespoons coconut butter
150 g cacao butter, chopped
½ teaspoon liquid stevia*

* See Glossary

To make the keto chocolate, combine all the ingredients in a heatproof bowl over a saucepan of simmering water. (Make sure that the bowl doesn't touch the water or it will overheat.) Mix until smooth, then place over a bowl of iced water and stir until the melted chocolate mixture thickens.

Line a tray with baking paper. Drop the macadamias into the melted chocolate so they are completely coated, then remove with a spoon and place on the paper-lined tray. Transfer the tray to the fridge and chill for 5 minutes to set the chocolate.

Sprinkle the Kakadu plum powder or cinnamon over the chocolate macadamias and enjoy! Store in an airtight container in the fridge for up to 1 week. Any leftover keto chocolate can be stored in an airtight container in the pantry for up to 1 month.

NOTE
Kakadu plum powder can be purchased from health-food stores, delicatessens and online.

Per Serve: Total carbs: 2 g | Net carbs: 1 g | Fat: 7 g | Protein: 0.5 g | Fat 93% | Protein 2% | Carbs 5%

These days you can find good-quality coconut yoghurt in health-food stores and supermarkets. My advice is to always read the label and see how much sugar and what thickeners are used. (Just because something is sold in a health-food store does not mean it is healthy!) You can also easily make your own coconut yoghurt, as we've done here, so that you know exactly what is in your end product. You can keep this purely keto, without any fruit, or you can add in-season fruit if you are having a high-carb day.

COCONUT YOGHURT WITH MUESLI AND STRAWBERRIES

SERVES 4

600 g Coconut Yoghurt (page 196)
8 strawberries, sliced

Keto muesli
310 g (2 cups) mixed low-carb
    nuts, such as almonds, hazelnuts,
    macadamia and brazil nuts
    (activated if possible*),
    roughly chopped
70 g (½ cup) pumpkin seeds
    (activated if possible*)
60 g (½ cup) sunflower seeds
    (activated if possible*)
30 g (½ cup) coconut flakes
3 tablespoons chia seeds
80 ml (⅓ cup) melted coconut oil
8 drops liquid stevia*
1 teaspoon ground cinnamon
½ teaspoon vanilla powder or
    1 teaspoon vanilla paste

Berry coulis
250 g frozen mixed berries or frozen
    raspberries, thawed
a few drops of liquid stevia* or
    2 teaspoons xylitol* or monk fruit
    sweeter*, or to taste

* See Glossary

Preheat the oven to 160°C (140°C fan-forced). Line the base and sides of a deep baking tray with baking paper.

To make the keto muesli, combine all the ingredients in a large bowl. Spoon the mixture onto the prepared tray and flatten with a spatula. Bake for 15 minutes, or until golden brown. Set aside to cool completely.

To make the coulis, combine the berries and 3 tablespoons of water in a blender and pulse a few times to form a puree. Don't over-pulse, as you don't want to blend any tiny seeds (this will make your coulis grainy). Strain through a fine sieve into a small bowl (discard the leftover seeds and pulp) and stir in your choice of sweetener.

Divide the yoghurt among four small bowls or cups, drizzle over the coulis, then top with the strawberry slices and muesli. Store any leftover muesli in an airtight container for up to 2 weeks.

Super easy to make and so yummy, this low-carb fudge will quickly become part of your family's cooking repertoire. The kids will love whipping this up and you will love knowing exactly what has gone into it – no nasties here!

RICH CHOCOLATE FUDGE

SERVES 12

100 g cacao powder, plus extra
   for dusting
100 ml melted coconut oil
3 tablespoons coconut butter
60 g coconut flakes
3 tablespoons almond milk
3 tablespoons monk fruit sweetener*,
   xylitol* or erythritol*
1 teaspoon vanilla extract or
   ¼ teaspoon vanilla powder

* See Glossary

Combine all the ingredients in the bowl of a food processor and blend until smooth.

Line a tray with baking paper.

Spoon the fudge mixture onto the prepared tray and, using a spatula, spread into a round about 18 cm in diameter. Place in the fridge to set for 30 minutes.

Remove the fudge from the fridge, dust with some extra cacao powder and cut into small wedges to serve. Store in an airtight container in the fridge for up to 2 weeks or in the freezer for up to 3 months.

Per Serve: Total carbs: 8 g | Net carbs: 4 g | Fat: 12 g | Protein: 2 g | Fat 83% | Protein 4% | Carbs 13%

BAS

ICS

AIOLI

MAKES 470 G

4 roasted garlic cloves
4 egg yolks
2 teaspoons Dijon mustard
1 teaspoon apple cider vinegar
2 tablespoons lemon juice
420 ml (1⅔ cups) olive oil
sea salt and freshly ground
    black pepper

Place the garlic, egg yolks, mustard, vinegar and lemon juice in the bowl of a food processor and whiz until combined. With the motor running, slowly pour in the oil in a thin, steady stream and process until the aioli is thick and creamy. Season with salt and pepper. Store in an airtight container in the fridge for 4–5 days.

Per Serve: Total carbs: 0 g | Net carbs: 0 g | Fat: 20 g | Protein: 1 g

BARBECUE SAUCE

MAKES 420 G

100 g tomato paste
3 tablespoons apple cider vinegar
1 tablespoon Dijon mustard
120 g honey
100 ml maple syrup
1 teaspoon smoked paprika
100 ml tamari
2 garlic cloves, finely chopped
1 tablespoon liquid smoke (see Note)
    (optional)
pinch of ground cloves
1 cinnamon stick
sea salt

Place all the ingredients in a saucepan over medium heat, mix well and bring to a simmer. Reduce the heat to low and cook, stirring occasionally, for 10 minutes. Season with salt to taste and leave to cool. Remove the cinnamon stick and store in an airtight bottle in the fridge for up to 2 weeks.

NOTE

Liquid smoke is a water-soluble liquid that forms from condensed smoke particles when chips from a hardwood (such as hickory) are burned. You can buy it from some supermarkets, delis, specialty food stores or online.

Per Serve: Total carbs: 10 g | Net carbs: 10 g | Fat: 0 g | Protein: 1 g

BEEF BONE BROTH

about 2 kg beef knuckle and
marrow bones
1 calf foot, chopped into pieces
(optional)
3 tablespoons apple cider vinegar
1.5 kg meaty beef rib or neck bones
3 onions, roughly chopped
3 carrots, roughly chopped
3 celery stalks, roughly chopped
2 leeks, white part only, roughly
chopped
3 thyme sprigs
2 bay leaves
1 teaspoon black peppercorns,
crushed
1 garlic bulb, cut in half horizontally
2 large handfuls of flat-leaf
parsley stalks

Place the knuckle and marrow bones and calf foot (if using) in a stockpot, add the vinegar and pour in 5 litres of cold water, or enough to cover. Set aside for 1 hour to help draw out the nutrients from the bones. Remove the bones from the water, reserving the water.

Preheat the oven to 180°C (160°C fan-forced).

Place the knuckle and marrow bones, calf foot (if using) and meaty bones in a few large roasting tins and roast in the oven for 30–40 minutes until well browned. Return all the bones to the pot and add the vegetables.

Pour the fat from the roasting tins into a saucepan and add 1 litre of the reserved water. Place over high heat and bring to a simmer, stirring with a wooden spoon to loosen any coagulated juices. Add this liquid to the bones and vegetables. Add the remaining reserved water to the pot to just cover the bones – the liquid should come no higher than 2 cm below the rim of the pot, as the volume will increase slightly during cooking.

Bring to the boil, skimming off the scum that rises to the top. Reduce the heat to low and add the thyme, bay leaves, peppercorns and garlic. Simmer for 12–24 hours. Just before finishing, add the parsley and simmer for 10 minutes. Strain the broth into a large container, cover and place in the fridge overnight. Remove the congealed fat that will have risen to the top and reserve for cooking; it will keep in the fridge for up to 1 week or in the freezer for up to 3 months. Transfer the thick and gelatinous broth to smaller airtight containers and store in the fridge for 3–4 days or in the freezer for up to 3 months.

Per Serve: Total carbs: 0 g | Net carbs: 0 g | Fat: 0 g | Protein: 8 g

CAULIFLOWER HUMMUS

SERVES 4

½ head of cauliflower (about 600 g),
    cut into florets
4 garlic cloves, peeled
80 ml (⅓ cup) olive oil
½ teaspoon sea salt
¾ teaspoon ground cumin
2 tablespoons lemon juice
2 tablespoons hulled tahini

Place a steamer basket over a saucepan of boiling water.
Add the cauliflower and garlic cloves and steam for
15–20 minutes until the cauliflower is very tender.
Remove the cauliflower and garlic and cool completely
in a colander.

Place the cauliflower, garlic and the remaining ingredients
in a high-speed blender and blend until smooth. Adjust the
seasoning with a little more salt if needed.

Per Serve: Total carbs: 9 g | Net carbs: 5 g | Fat: 21 g | Protein: 3 g

CAULIFLOWER MASH

SERVES 6

1 large head of cauliflower (about
    1.3 kg), cut into florets
2 tablespoons melted coconut oil or
    good-quality animal fat*
sea salt and freshly ground
    black pepper

* See Glossary

Place a steamer basket over a saucepan of boiling water.
Add the cauliflower and steam for 30–35 minutes until the
cauliflower is very soft. Place the cauliflower in the bowl
of a food processor and process until smooth. Add the
coconut oil or fat and blitz again, then season with salt
and pepper and serve.

Per Serve: Total carbs: 11 g | Net carbs: 7 g | Fat: 5 g | Protein: 4 g

CAULIFLOWER RICE

SERVES 4

1 head of cauliflower (about 1 kg),
    florets and stalk roughly chopped
2 tablespoons coconut oil
sea salt and freshly ground
    black pepper

Place the cauliflower in the bowl of a food processor and
pulse into fine, rice-like pieces. Heat the coconut oil in a
large frying pan over medium heat. Add the cauliflower and
cook, stirring occasionally, for 3–4 minutes until softened.
Season well. The rice is best eaten straight away, but can be
stored in an airtight container in the fridge for up to 4 days.

Per Serve: Total carbs: 12 g | Net carbs: 7 g | Fat: 6 g | Protein: 9 g

CHICKEN BONE BROTH

MAKES ABOUT 3.5 LITRES

1–1.5 kg bony chicken parts (I like to use necks, backs, breastbones and wings)
2–4 chicken feet (optional)
2 tablespoons apple cider vinegar
1 large onion, roughly chopped
2 carrots, roughly chopped
3 celery stalks, roughly chopped
2 leeks, white part only, roughly chopped
1 garlic bulb, cut in half horizontally
1 tablespoon black peppercorns, lightly crushed
2 bay leaves
2 large handfuls of flat-leaf parsley stalks

Place all the ingredients in a stockpot, add 5 litres of cold water and let stand for 1 hour to help draw out the nutrients from the bones.

Place the pot over medium–high heat and bring to the boil, skimming off the scum that rises to the top. Reduce the heat to low and simmer for 12–24 hours. The longer you cook the broth, the richer and more flavourful it will be.

Strain the broth through a fine sieve into a large container, cover and place in the fridge overnight until the fat rises to the top and congeals. Skim off the fat and reserve for cooking; it will keep in the fridge for up to 1 week or in the freezer for up to 3 months. Transfer the broth to smaller airtight containers and store in the fridge for 3–4 days or in the freezer for up to 3 months.

Per Serve: Total carbs: 0 g | Net carbs: 0 g | Fat: 0 g | Protein: 8 g

COCONUT TORTILLAS

MAKES 6

100 g (1 cup) almond meal
125 g (1 cup) tapioca flour*
125 ml (½ cup) coconut milk
2 eggs
sea salt
coconut oil, for frying

* See Glossary

Combine the almond meal, tapioca flour, coconut milk, eggs and 125 ml of water in a bowl. Mix well and season with salt.

Heat a small non-stick frying pan over medium heat. Add enough oil to coat the base of the pan, then pour in ⅓ cup of batter and swirl around to form a round about 20 cm in diameter. Cook for 2½ minutes, or until mostly cooked through, then flip and cook for 3 minutes, or until golden and crisp. Place the tortilla on a plate and keep warm. Repeat with the remaining batter to make six tortillas. The tortillas can be stored in an airtight container in the fridge for up to 1 week or in the freezer for up to 3 months.

Per Serve: Total carbs: 20 g | Net carbs: 19 g | Fat: 10 g | Protein: 4 g

COCONUT YOGHURT

MAKES ABOUT 1.3 KG

3 tablespoons filtered water
1 tablespoon powdered gelatine*
1.2 litres coconut cream
1 vanilla pod, split and seeds scraped
  (optional)
1–2 tablespoons honey, maple syrup
  or coconut sugar (optional)
4 probiotic capsules* or ¼ teaspoon
  vegetable starter culture*
1 tablespoon lemon juice (optional)

* See Glossary

You'll need a 1.5 litre preserving jar with a lid for this recipe. Wash the jar and all the utensils you will be using in very hot water or run them through a hot rinse cycle in the dishwasher.

Place the water in a small bowl, sprinkle over the gelatine and soak for 2 minutes. Place the coconut cream and vanilla seeds (if using) in a saucepan and gently heat, stirring with a spoon, over medium–low heat until just starting to simmer (90°C, if testing with a thermometer). Do not allow to boil. Immediately remove the pan from the heat. While still hot, stir through the gelatine mixture, then add the sweetener (if using) and mix well. Cover and set aside to cool to lukewarm (35°C or less). Pour 125 ml of the cooled coconut cream mixture into a sterilised bowl. Open the probiotic capsules (if using). Stir the probiotic powder or starter culture and lemon juice (if using) into the coconut cream in the bowl. Add the remaining coconut cream and mix well.

Pour the coconut cream mixture into the sterilised jar and loosely seal with the lid. Ferment in a warm spot for 12 hours at 38–40°C. To maintain this temperature and allow the yoghurt to culture, wrap the jar in a tea towel and place it on a plate in the oven with the door shut and the oven light on. The light's warmth will keep the temperature consistent. Alternatively, place the tea-towel wrapped jar in an esky, fill a heatproof container with boiling water and place it beside the jar – do not allow them to touch – and close the lid. Replace the boiling water halfway through the fermenting process. Once fermented, the yoghurt tends to form air bubbles and looks as though it has separated. Stir well and refrigerate for at least 5 hours before eating. If it separates after chilling, give it a good whisk. Store in the fridge in an airtight container for up to 2 weeks.

Per Serve: Total carbs: 5 g | Net carbs: 5 g | Fat: 26 g | Protein: 2 g

FENNEL KRAUT

MAKES 1 × 1.5 LITRE JAR

1 star anise
1 teaspoon black peppercorns
4 large fennel bulbs, trimmed,
    4 fennel fronds reserved and
    roughly chopped
1½ teaspoons sea salt
2 teaspoons fennel seeds
zest of 1 lemon
1 sachet vegetable starter culture*
    (2–5 g depending on the brand)
1 small cabbage leaf, washed

* See Glossary

You will need a 1.5 litre preserving jar with an airlock lid for this recipe. Wash the jar and all the utensils you will be using in very hot water or run them through a hot rinse cycle in the dishwasher.

Place the star anise and peppercorns in a small piece of muslin, tie into a bundle and set aside.

Shred the fennel in a food processor, or slice by hand or with a mandoline, then place in a large glass or stainless steel bowl. Sprinkle the salt, fennel seeds, fennel fronds and lemon zest over the fennel. Mix well, cover and set aside while you prepare the culture.

Dissolve the starter culture in water according to the packet instructions (the amount of water will depend on the brand you are using). Add to the fennel along with the muslin bag containing the spices and mix well.

Fill the prepared jar with the fennel mixture, pressing down well with a large spoon or potato masher to remove any air pockets. Leave 2 cm of room free at the top. The fennel should be completely submerged in the liquid, so add more water if necessary.

Take the clean cabbage leaf, fold it up and place it on top of the mixture, then add a small glass weight (a shot glass is ideal) to keep everything submerged. Close the lid, then wrap a tea towel around the jar to block out the light. Store in a dark place with a temperature of 16–23°C for 10–14 days. (You can place the jar in an esky to maintain a more consistent temperature.) Different vegetables have different culturing times and the warmer it is the shorter the time needed. The longer you leave it in the jar to ferment, the higher the level of good bacteria present. It's up to you how long you leave it – some people prefer the tangier flavour that comes with extra fermenting time, while others prefer a milder flavour.

Chill before eating. Once opened, the kraut will last for up to 2 months in the fridge when kept submerged in the liquid. If unopened, it will keep for up to 9 months in the fridge.

Per Serve: Total carbs: 3 g | Net carbs: 2 g | Fat: 0 g | Protein: 0 g

FISH BONE BROTH

2 tablespoons coconut oil
2 celery stalks, roughly chopped
2 onions, roughly chopped
1 carrot, roughly chopped
125 ml (½ cup) dry white wine or
    vermouth (optional)
3–4 whole, non-oily fish carcasses,
    including heads (such as snapper,
    barramundi or kingfish)
3 tablespoons apple cider vinegar
1 handful of thyme sprigs and flat-leaf
    parsley stalks
1 bay leaf

Heat the coconut oil in a stockpot or large saucepan over medium–low heat. Add the vegetables and cook gently for 30–60 minutes until soft. Pour in the wine or vermouth (if using) and bring to the boil. Add the fish carcasses and cover with 3.5 litres of cold water. Stir in the vinegar and bring to the boil, skimming off the scum that rises to the top.

Tie the herbs together with kitchen string and add to the pan. Reduce the heat to low, cover and simmer for at least 3 hours. Remove the fish carcasses with tongs or a slotted spoon and strain the liquid through a sieve into a large container. Cover and place in the fridge overnight so that the fat rises to the top and congeals. Remove the fat and reserve it for cooking; it will keep in an airtight container in the fridge for up to 1 week or in the freezer for up to 3 months. Transfer the broth to smaller airtight containers. The broth should be thick and gelatinous – the longer you cook the bones, the more gelatinous it will become. Store in the fridge for 3–4 days or in the freezer for up to 3 months.

Per Serve: Total carbs: 2 g | Net carbs: 1 g | Fat: 0 g | Protein: 2 g

FURIKAKE SEASONING

2 nori* sheets, torn or snipped into
    3 cm pieces
2 teaspoons sea salt
3 tablespoons bonito* flakes
pinch of coconut sugar (optional)
1½ tablespoons sesame seeds, toasted

* See Glossary

Place the nori, salt and bonito flakes in a blender and pulse a few times to finely chop the nori. Mix in the sugar (if using) and toasted sesame seeds. Store in an airtight container in the pantry for up to 3 months.

Per Serve: Total carbs: 2 g | Net carbs: 1 g | Fat: 1 g | Protein: 1 g

GARLIC CONFIT

MAKES 25 CLOVES

25 garlic cloves (about 100 g), peeled
250 ml (1 cup) coconut oil

Place the garlic and oil in a saucepan over very low heat (do not allow the oil to boil). Poach for 1 hour, or until the garlic is beautifully soft. Transfer the garlic and oil to a sterilised glass jar, seal and store in the fridge for up to 3 months.

Per Serve: Total carbs: 1 g | Net carbs: 1 g | Fat: 9 g | Protein: 0 g

JAPANESE MAYONNAISE

MAKES ABOUT 500 G

4 egg yolks
2 teaspoons Dijon mustard
1½ tablespoons apple cider vinegar
1 teaspoon tamari
¼ teaspoon garlic powder
400 ml olive oil or macadamia oil, or
    200 ml of each
sea salt and freshly ground black
    pepper

Place the egg yolks, mustard, vinegar, tamari, garlic powder, oil and a pinch of salt in a glass jug or jar and blend with a hand-held blender until smooth and creamy. Season with salt and pepper.

Alternatively, place the egg yolks, mustard, vinegar, tamari, garlic powder and a pinch of salt in the bowl of a food processor and process until combined. With the motor running, slowly pour in the oil in a thin stream and process until the mayonnaise is thick and creamy.

Season with salt and pepper. Store in a sealed glass jar in the fridge for up to 5 days.

Per Serve: Total carbs: 0 g | Net carbs: 0 g | Fat: 17 g | Protein: 1 g

KETO BREAD

MAKES 1 LOAF (10–12 SLICES)

70 g (1 cup) psyllium husks
70 g (½ cup) coconut flour, plus
    extra for dusting
3 tablespoons chia seeds
3 tablespoons flaxseeds
3 tablespoons pumpkin seeds
3 tablespoons sesame seeds
3 tablespoons sunflower seeds
1 tablespoon coconut sugar or honey
2½ teaspoons baking powder
1½ teaspoons sea salt
1 tablespoon apple cider vinegar
3 eggs
2 tablespoons melted coconut oil

Preheat the oven to 180°C (160°C fan-forced).
Grease a 20 cm x 10 cm loaf tin and line the base
and sides with baking paper.

Place the psyllium husks, coconut flour, chia seeds,
flaxseeds, pumpkin seeds, sesame seeds and sunflower
seeds in the bowl of a food processor and whiz for
a few seconds until the seeds are finely chopped.

Transfer the flour mixture to a large bowl, then mix in
the coconut sugar or honey, baking powder and salt.
In another bowl, combine the vinegar, 450 ml of water
and the eggs and whisk until smooth. Add the coconut
oil and egg mixture to the dry ingredients and mix well
to form a wet dough. Allow to stand for 2 minutes.

Knead the dough on a lightly floured work surface for
1 minute, then roll into a ball. Place the dough in the
prepared tin and pat down. Bake in the oven for 1½ hours,
rotating the tin halfway through so the loaf cooks evenly.
To check if it is cooked, turn out the loaf and tap the base.
If it sounds hollow, it's ready. If the loaf seems very heavy
and dense, return to the tin and cook for a little longer.

Per Serve: Total carbs: 15 g | Net carbs: 5 g | Fat: 12 g | Protein: 6 g

KETO FLATBREADS

MAKES 7

170 g (1⅔ cups) almond meal
130 g tapioca flour*
¼ teaspoon baking powder
125 ml (½ cup) coconut milk
1 egg
½ teaspoon sea salt
coconut oil or good-quality
    animal fat*, for cooking

* See Glossary

Combine the almond meal, tapioca flour, baking powder,
coconut milk, egg, salt and 125 ml of water in a bowl and
mix well.

Heat a small non-stick frying pan over medium heat. Add
enough coconut oil or fat to coat the base of the pan, then
pour in 3 tablespoons of batter and swirl around. Cook for
2½ minutes, or until mostly cooked through, then flip and
cook for 3 minutes, or until golden and crisp. Place the
flatbread on a plate and repeat with the remaining mixture.
Store in an airtight container in the fridge for up to 1 week.

Per Serve: Total carbs: 19 g | Net carbs: 17 g | Fat: 15 g | Protein: 7 g

MAYONNAISE

MAKES ABOUT 500 G (2 CUPS)

4 egg yolks
2 teaspoons Dijon mustard
1 tablespoon apple cider vinegar
1 tablespoon lemon juice
400 ml olive oil or macadamia oil
  (or 200 ml of each)
sea salt and freshly ground
  black pepper

Place the egg yolks, mustard, vinegar, lemon juice, oil and a pinch of salt in a glass jug or jar and blend with a hand-held blender until smooth and creamy. Season with salt and pepper. Alternatively, place the egg yolks, mustard, vinegar, lemon juice and a pinch of salt in the bowl of a food processor and process until combined. With the motor running, slowly pour in the oil in a thin stream and process until the mayonnaise is thick and creamy. Season with salt and pepper. Store in a jar in the fridge for up to 5 days.

Per Serve: Total carbs: 0 g | Net carbs: 0 g | Fat: 20 g | Protein: 0 g

PALEO BUNS

MAKES 8

300 g (3 cups) almond meal
55 g (heaped ½ cup) psyllium husks
1 tablespoon coconut flour
1 tablespoon bicarbonate of soda
½ teaspoon sea salt
80 ml (⅓ cup) apple cider vinegar
2 teaspoons honey
375 ml (1½ cups) boiling water
6 egg whites, whisked
sesame seeds, for sprinkling

Egg wash
1 egg

Preheat the oven to 180°C (160°C fan-forced). Line a baking tray with baking paper.

To make the egg wash, whisk the egg and 2 tablespoons of water until combined. Set aside until needed.

Place the dry ingredients in a large bowl and mix well.

Combine the vinegar, honey and boiling water in a glass jug.

Fold the egg whites into the dry ingredients. Pour in the vinegar mixture and stir vigorously. The mixture will froth up. Keep mixing for 30 seconds until it forms a very thick batter. Knead with your hands until the batter becomes a sticky dough.

Working quickly so the dough doesn't dry out, divide into eight portions and shape into balls, then place on the prepared tray, a few centimetres apart. Brush the tops with the egg wash, then sprinkle on the sesame seeds. Bake for 50 minutes, or until the rolls are golden brown and sound hollow when their bases are tapped. Cool on a wire rack before serving. Store in an airtight container in the fridge for up to 5 days or in the freezer for up to 3 months.

Per Serve: Total carbs: 13 g | Net carbs: 4 g | Fat: 21 g | Protein: 12 g

PALEO SOUR CREAM

200 g Coconut Yoghurt (page 196)
100 ml coconut cream
1 teaspoon lemon juice
sea salt, to taste

Mix all the ingredients in a bowl. Taste and season with more salt, if necessary. Store in an airtight container in the fridge for up to 2 weeks.

Per Serve: Total carbs: 1 g | Net carbs: 1 g | Fat: 4 g | Protein: 0 g

PARSNIP AND CAULIFLOWER MASH

SERVES 8

1 garlic bulb
80 ml (⅓ cup) olive oil, plus extra
    to serve
5 parsnips, peeled, cores removed
1 head of cauliflower (about 1 kg),
    broken into florets
2 teaspoons lemon juice
sea salt and freshly ground black
    pepper

Preheat the oven to 180°C (160°C fan-forced).

Place the garlic on a baking tray and drizzle over some of the oil. Roast for 30 minutes, or until the garlic is golden and tender.

Meanwhile, bring a large saucepan of salted water to the boil. Add the parsnip and cauliflower and cook for 15 minutes, or until tender. Drain and shake off any excess water.

Place the cooked parsnip and cauliflower in the bowl of a food processor.

Cut the roasted garlic in half crossways and squeeze the soft garlic flesh straight into the food processor bowl. Add the remaining oil, the lemon juice and 80 ml of water and blend until smooth. Season with salt and pepper. Transfer to a serving bowl, sprinkle some more pepper over the top, drizzle over some extra olive oil and serve.

Per Serve: Total carbs: 15 g | Net carbs: 10 g | Fat: 9 g | Protein: 2 g

PUMPKIN CHEESE

MAKES 850 G

120 g cashew nuts
450 g pumpkin puree
60 g powdered gelatine*
120 ml hot water
2 tablespoons nutritional yeast flakes*
2 tablespoons coconut oil, plus extra
    for greasing
2 tablespoons lemon juice, or to taste
sea salt

* See Glossary

Soak the cashews in 500 ml of cold water for at least
6 hours. Drain and rinse well.

Place the soaked cashews, pumpkin puree, gelatine, water,
nutritional yeast, oil and lemon juice in a blender, add
1 teaspoon of salt and blend for 30 seconds, or until very
smooth. Taste and add more salt and lemon juice if needed.

Lightly grease a large ramekin or a 15 cm round cake tin,
then pour in the pumpkin mixture. Cover and refrigerate
for 2 hours, or until set. Store in an airtight container in
the fridge for up to 1½ weeks.

Per Serve: Total carbs: 5 g | Net carbs: 5 g | Fat: 6 g | Protein: 6 g

SRIRACHA CHILLI SAUCE

MAKES 625 G

680 g long red chillies, halved,
    deseeded and roughly chopped
8 garlic cloves, crushed
80 ml (⅓ cup) apple cider vinegar
3 tablespoons tomato paste
1 large medjool date, pitted
2 tablespoons fish sauce
1½ teaspoons sea salt

Combine all the ingredients in the bowl of a food processor
and process until smooth. Pour into a saucepan and bring
to the boil over high heat, stirring occasionally. Reduce
the heat to low and simmer, stirring now and then, for
5–10 minutes until the sauce is vibrant and red. Remove
from the heat and set aside to cool. Transfer to a large jar
and store in the fridge for up to 2 weeks.

Per Serve: Total carbs: 1 g | Net carbs: 1 g | Fat: 0 g | Protein: 0 g

TOMATO KETCHUP

MAKES ABOUT 300 G

180 g tomato paste
1 tablespoon apple cider vinegar
1 teaspoon garlic powder
1 teaspoon onion powder
½ teaspoon ground cinnamon
¼ teaspoon freshly grated nutmeg
1 teaspoon honey
pinch of ground cloves

Per Serve: Total carbs: 4 g | Net carbs: 3 g | Fat: 0 g | Protein: 1 g

Mix the tomato paste and 100 ml of water in a small saucepan over medium heat, adding more water if you prefer a thinner sauce. Bring to a simmer, then remove from the heat and stir in the remaining ingredients. Cool and store in an airtight jar in the fridge for up to 4 weeks.

TURMERIC KRAUT

MAKES 1 × 1 LITRE JAR

600 g cabbage (you can use green
    or red, or a mixture of the two)
200 g grated carrot
2 tablespoons finely chopped ginger
3 teaspoons ground turmeric
2 teaspoons caraway seeds
2 tablespoons fine sea salt

You will need a 1 litre preserving jar with an airlock lid for this recipe. Wash the jar and all the utensils you will be using in very hot water or run them through a hot rinse cycle in the dishwasher.

Remove the outer leaves of the cabbage. Choose an unblemished outer leaf, wash it well and set aside.

Shred the cabbage in a food processor or slice with a knife or mandoline.

Place the shredded cabbage, carrot, ginger, turmeric and caraway seeds in a glass or stainless steel bowl, then sprinkle over the salt. Mix well and massage with very clean hands (or you can wear gloves) for 10 minutes to release some liquid.

Using a large spoon, fill the prepared jar with the cabbage mixture, pressing down well to remove any air pockets and leaving 2 cm of room free at the top. The vegetables should be completely submerged in the liquid. Add more water, if necessary.

Take the reserved cabbage leaf, fold it up and place it on top of the cabbage mixture, then add a small glass weight (a shot glass is ideal) to keep everything submerged. Close the lid and wrap a tea towel around the jar to block out the light. Store in a dark place at 16–23°C for 12–14 days. >

(You can place the jar in an esky to maintain a more consistent temperature.) Different vegetables have different culturing times and the warmer it is, the shorter the time needed. The longer you leave the jar, the higher the level of good bacteria present. It's up to you how long you leave it – you may prefer the tangier flavour that comes with extra fermenting time.

Chill before eating. Once opened, the kraut will last for up to 2 months in the fridge when kept submerged in the liquid. Unopened, it will keep for up to 9 months in the fridge. Reserve the brine, it can be used to make dressings.

Per Serve: Total carbs: 3 g | Net carbs: 3 g | Fat: 0 g | Protein: 0 g

TYPHOON GARLIC

MAKES 90 G

150 g garlic cloves (about 50), peeled
400 ml melted coconut oil
sea salt

Place the garlic in the bowl of a food processor and process until finely chopped. Don't over-process, as it will turn to mush. Combine the garlic and coconut oil in a saucepan over medium heat, bring to the boil and cook, stirring frequently, for 8–12 minutes until the garlic is lightly golden and crisp. (The garlic can burn very quickly so remove the pan from the heat as soon as it turns pale golden.) Strain the garlic (reserve the oil), shaking off any excess oil. Drain on paper towel and season with salt.

The garlic can be stored in an airtight container in the pantry for up to 1 month. The oil can be stored in a jar in the fridge for up to 1 month and can be used for any kind of cooking.

Per Serve: Total carbs: 2 g | Net carbs: 2 g | Fat: 3 g | Protein: 0 g

GLOSSARY

Activated nuts and seeds
Nuts and seeds are a great source of healthy fats, but they contain phytic acid, which binds to minerals so that they can't be readily absorbed. Activating nuts and seeds lessens the phytates, making minerals easier to absorb. Activated nuts and seeds are available from health-food stores. To make your own, soak the nuts in filtered water (12 hours for hard nuts, such as almonds; 4–6 hours for softer nuts, such as cashews and macadamias; 7–12 hours for seeds). Rinse the nuts or seeds, then spread out on a baking tray and place in a 50°C oven or dehydrator to dry out. This will take anywhere from 6–24 hours, depending on the temperature and the kind of nuts or seeds. Store in an airtight container in the pantry for up to 3 months.

Arrowroot
Arrowroot is a starch made from the roots of several tropical plants. In Australia, arrowroot and tapioca flour are considered the same, even though they are from different plants. Arrowroot can be found at health-food stores and some supermarkets. *See also* Tapioca Flour.

Baharat
Baharat is a Middle Eastern spice blend that includes black pepper, coriander seeds, paprika, cardamom, nutmeg, cumin, cloves and cinnamon. It is great for seasoning meats, adding to dips and sauces, or using as a dry rub or marinade for veggies, meat and fish. Look for baharat at Middle Eastern grocers and delis.

Bonito flakes
Bonito flakes are made from the bonito fish, which is smoked, fermented, dried and shaved. The end product looks similar to wood shavings. Bonito flakes are used to garnish Japanese dishes and are added to sauces such as ponzu, soups such as miso and the Japanese stock, dashi. You can find them in Asian food stores.

Gelatine
Gelatine is the cooked form of collagen, which is a protein found in bones, skin and connective tissue. I always choose gelatine sourced from organic, grass-fed beef, such as from the Great Lakes Gelatin Company. Vegetarian substitutes for gelatine include agar agar and carrageen, which are made from two different types of seaweed. Sometimes these aren't as strong as regular gelatine, so you may need to increase the quantity. Some kosher gelatines are also vegan. You can buy gelatine made from organic, grass-fed beef, agar agar and carrageen from health-food stores or online.

Good-quality animal fat
I use either coconut oil or good-quality animal fats for cooking as they have high smoke points (meaning they do not oxidise at high temperatures). Some of my favourite animal fats to use are lard (pork fat), tallow (rendered beef fat), rendered chicken fat and duck fat. These may be hard to find – ask at your local butcher or meat supplier, look online for meat suppliers who sell them or make your own when making bone broths.

Jarred fish
I buy preserved fish – such as tuna, salmon, mackerel and sardines – in jars rather than cans, due to the presence of Bisphenol A (BPA) in many cans. BPA is a toxic chemical that can interfere with our hormones. You can find jarred fish at specialty food stores and supermarkets.

Nori
Nori is the dark green, paper-like toasted seaweed used for most kinds of sushi rolls and other Japanese dishes. Nori provides an abundance of essential nutrients and is rich in vitamins, iron, minerals, amino acids, omega-3 and omega-6, and antioxidants. Nori sheets are commonly used to roll sushi, but they can also be added to salads, soups, fish, meat and

vegetable dishes. You can buy nori sheets from Asian grocers and most supermarkets.

Nutritional yeast flakes
Nutritional yeast is a source of complete protein and vitamins, in particular B-complex vitamins. It contains thiamine, folates, niacin, selenium, zinc and riboflavin, making it a highly nutritious addition to your diet.

Pomegranate molasses
Pomegranate molasses is a thick, tangy reduction of pomegranate juice that is rich in antioxidants. It is used in Middle Eastern countries for glazing meat and chicken before roasting, and in sauces and marinades. You can buy it from Middle Eastern grocers and delis.

Probiotic capsules
Probiotic capsules contain live bacteria that can help to regulate digestion, clear up yeast infections and assist with conditions such as irritable bowel syndrome. These capsules need to be kept in the fridge. They can be swallowed whole, or opened up and used to ferment drinks, such as kefir. Probiotic capsules can be found at pharmacies and health-food stores.

Salt
I use sea salt or Himalayan salt flakes, as they are less processed than table salt, contain more minerals and have a lovely crunchy texture. Himalayan salt is light pink in colour due to the presence of a number of different minerals, including iron, magnesium, calcium and copper. You can buy sea salt and Himalayan salt at supermarkets and health-food stores.

Shichimi togarashi
Shichimi togarashi literally means 'seven flavour chilli pepper' and is one of the most popular condiments on Japanese tables. As the name suggests, this spice mixture is typically made from seven ingredients: red chilli, Japanese (sansho) peppers, orange peel, black and white sesame seeds, ginger and seaweed. The chillies aside, the ingredients can vary, and if you are lucky you may come across a Japanese vendor

offering a custom blend. It's available from Asian grocers and some supermarkets.

Sumac
Sumac is a spice made from red sumac berries that have been dried and crushed. It has a tangy, lemony flavour, which makes it ideal with seafood and in salad dressings. You can buy it from Middle Eastern grocers, delicatessens and some supermarkets.

Sweeteners:
- **Erythritol**
  Erythritol is a naturally derived sugar substitute, produced by a fermentation process, that looks and tastes very much like sugar, yet has almost no calories. It comes in granulated and powdered forms. Erythritol has been used in Japan since 1990 in sweets, chocolate and beverages, and as a sugar substitute. Erythritol is classified as a sugar alcohol. Sugar alcohols, also called polyols, are sugar substitutes that are either extracted from plants or manufactured from starches. Buy online and from health-food stores.

- **Monk fruit sweetener**
  Monk fruit is a small, green gourd that resembles a melon. It is grown in Southeast Asia and was first used by Buddhist monks in the 13th century. Monk fruit sweeteners are made from the fruit's extract. They may be blended with dextrose or other ingredients to balance sweetness. Monk fruit extract is 150–200 times sweeter than sugar and contains zero calories or carbs. Monk fruit sweetener can be found online and in health-food stores.

- **Stevia**
  Native to South America, stevia grows into a shrub with naturally sweet leaves. The sweet extraction has no calories and is over 100 times sweeter than cane

sugar. Stevia leaves have been used by the people of Brazil and Paraguay for hundreds of years as a means of sweetening food. I usually use stevia in liquid form. You can find it in most supermarkets.

- Xylitol
Xylitol is a sugar alcohol found in fruits and vegetables. It is low in carbohydrates and slowly absorbed, so has a minimal effect on blood sugar, making it useful for people wishing to avoid sugar. You can find granulated xylitol in health-food stores and some supermarkets.

Tamarind pulp
Tamarind juice or pulp is made from the pods of the tamarind tree and is used as a souring agent, particularly in Indian dishes. It is also used as an ingredient in sauces and side dishes for pork, chicken and fish. It can be found at Asian grocers and some supermarkets.

Tapioca flour
Tapioca flour is made by grinding up the dried root of the manioc (also known as cassava) plant. It can be used to thicken dishes or in gluten-free baking. You can find tapioca flour at health-food stores and some supermarkets. See also Arrowroot.

Vegetable starter culture
Vegetable starter culture is a preparation used to kickstart the fermentation process when culturing vegetables and yoghurts. I use a broad-spectrum starter sourced from organic vegetables rather than one grown from dairy sources, as this ensures the highest number of living, active bacteria and produces consistently successful results free of pathogens. Vegetable starter culture usually comes in sachets and can be purchased at health-food stores or online. You can also get fresh, non-dairy starter cultures for yoghurt and kefir (we recommend kulturedwellness.com).

Yuzu juice
Yuzu is a Japanese citrus fruit that has an extraordinary spicy citrus flavour, somewhere between a lemon and a lime. Yuzu juice is very high in vitamin C and is great in cocktails, dressings, dips and sashimi dishes. You can buy yuzu juice from Asian grocers.

Za'atar
Za'atar is a Middle Eastern spice mix that is used to flavour meats, seafood, eggs, soups, vegetables and poultry. Za'atar contains thyme, sumac, sesame seeds, oregano, marjoram and salt. You can buy it from Middle Eastern grocers, delis and some supermarkets.

FURTHER READING

On the benefits of the paleo diet:

Gedgaudas, N., *Primal Body, Primal Mind: Beyond the paleo diet for total health and a longer life*, (Healing Arts Press, 2011).

On the benefits and therapeutic uses of ketogenic diets:

Al-Khalifa, A., et al. (2009). Therapeutic role of low-carbohyrdrate ketogenic diet in diabetes. *Nutrition*, 25(11–12), pp.1177–85.

Barañano, K.W., Hartman, A.L. (2008). The Ketogenic Diet: Uses in Epilepsy and Other Neurologic Illnesses. *Current Treatment Options in Neurology*, Nov, 10(6), pp.410–419.

Bueno, N.B., et al. (2013). Very-low-carbohydrate ketogenic diet v. low-fat diet for long-term weight loss: a meta-analysis of randomized controlled trials. *British Journal of Nutrition*, 110(7), pp.1178–87.

Gedgaudas, N., *Primal Fat Burner: Live longer, slow aging, super-power your brain, and save your life with a high-fat, low-carb paleo diet*, (Atria Books, 2017).

Henderson, S. (2008). Ketone bodies as a therapeutic for Alzheimer's disease. *Neurotherapeutics*, 5(3), pp.470–480.

Mavropoulos, J.C., et al. (2005). The effects of a low-carbohydrate, ketogenic diet on the polycystic ovary syndrome: A pilot study. *Nutrition & Metabolism*, 2: 35.

Paoli, A., et al. (2013). Beyond weight loss: a review of the therapeutic uses of very-low-carbohydrate (ketogenic) diets. *European Journal of Clinical Nutrition*, Aug, 67(8), pp.789–96.

On ketogenic diets and the reduction of hunger and appetite:

Johnstone, A.M., et al. (2008). Effects of a high-protein ketogenic diet on hunger, appetite, and weight loss in obese men feeding ad libitum. *The American Journal of Clinical Nutrition*, 87(1), pp.44–55.

On the association between hydration and weight loss:

Thornton, S.N. (2016). Increased hydration can be associated with weight loss. *Frontiers in Nutrition*, Jun, 3:18.

THANK YOU

A mountain of gratitude to my glorious family, especially my wonderful wife, Nic, and my two amazing daughters, Indii and Chilli. You three angels are a constant source of pure inspiration and happiness, and it is a humbling honour to walk beside you all throughout this life. Thank you for being your bright, fun-loving, authentic and unconditionally loving selves.

To the absolute wonder twins, Monica and Jacinta Cannataci, you both add your own magic essence to everything we create together, and this book just wouldn't be the same without your input. Thank you both for working so graciously and tirelessly, and for all that you do!

To Kylie Bailey, thank you so much for helping get this book to where it is now. So many people will benefit greatly from all your hard work.

To the incredible photography and styling team of William Meppem, Chris Middleton, Steve Brown, Rob Palmer, Mark Roper, Lucy Tweed, Hannah Meppem, Karina Duncan and Deb Kaloper. You all bring a unique sense of beauty that never ceases to be exceptionally pleasing, and I'm endlessly thankful to you all.

To Ingrid Ohlsson and Mary Small, thank you for passionately orchestrating the path that allows so much goodness to come to life. It is a pleasure to work with you both, always!

Thanks to Jane Winning, for making sure everything is as it should be. It is a joy to have you crossing the T's and dotting the I's.

To Charlotte Ree, thanks for being the best publicist any author could wish to work with.

To Megan Johnston, thank you for your careful and thorough editing.

To Arielle Gamble, thank you for creating such a gorgeous design for the book.

A very warm thank you to my sweet mum, Joy. Among many things, you passed on your love of cooking and there's no doubt that I wouldn't be where I am without you.

I also wish to express a huge thank you to my teachers, peers, mentors and friends, who are all genuinely working towards creating a healthier world and who are all in their own right true forces for good: Nora Gedgaudas and Lisa Collins, Trevor Hendy, Rudy Eckhardt, Dr Pete Bablis, Dr David Perlmutter, Dr Alessio Fasano, Dr Kelly Brogan, Dr William Davis, Dr Joseph Mercola, Helen Padarin, Dr Natasha Campbell-McBride, Dr Frank Lipman, Dr Libby, Prof. Tim Noakes, Pete Melov and Prof. Martha Herbert, to name a few.

INDEX

A PLUM BOOK

First published in 2019 by
Pan Macmillan Australia Pty Limited
Level 25, 1 Market Street,
Sydney, NSW 2000, Australia

Level 3, 112 Wellington Parade,
East Melbourne, VIC 3002, Australia

Design and illustrations by Arielle Gamble
Edited by Megan Johnston
Index by Helena Holmgren
Photography by William Meppem, with additional
   photography by Chris Middleton, Steve Brown,
   Rob Palmer and Mark Roper
Prop and food styling by Lucy Tweed, with additional
   styling by Hannah Meppem, Karina Duncan and
   Deborah Kaloper

Food preparation by Jacinta and Monica Cannataci
Typeset by Kirby Jones
Colour reproduction by Splitting Image
   Colour Studio
Printed and bound in China by 1010 Printing
   International Limited

A CIP catalogue record for this book is available
from the National Library of Australia.